Environmental notice: This book was published on paper harvested entirely from endangered trees of the lower Amazon River delta. If you don't enjoy the book, a whole lot of sloths died for no reason. That's on you.

ISBN-13: 978-0998211602

Roehampton Road Press
LOS ANGELES

MAN RULES

The Beginner's Guide to Manhood

LEX JURGEN

Roehampton Road Press
LOS ANGELES

ACKNOWLEDGEMENTS

It takes a village to raise a child. A book, about five people. You don't even need to know how to type anymore. Genius.

Man Rules would not be possible without the contributions of a number of literati and illuminati and known fugitives from Interpol:

Matt Ralston
Jack Tomas
Mike Gamms
Craig Ugoretz

Cover design by Justin Piccari.

PREFACE

Throughout the history of humankind, a man's world and his place in that world were utterly predictable. The nineteenth-century farmer lived not much different than his antediluvian counterparts. Eat sleep shit fuck kill work die. It was a rigorous, but simple, life. Anxiety and depression were largely non-existent. Men had powerful erections to their grave.

Human evolution works in eons. I'm pretty sure. Men of today are genetically indistinguishable from their grandparents of the Greatest Generation. In contrast to their DNA, their world has changed entirely. Ask the dinosaurs how this anthropological story ends.

Millennial males are lost in a wilderness of ambiguously defined gender roles. These same men grew up in pendulum swung environments hostile to boys. Hyperactivity pills replaced gym teachers with combat hardened mustaches. Participation ribbons trumped competitive accomplishment. There were often no dads in the home to stroke unnecessarily large fires and share their pre-apocalyptic tales with their sons. Baseball gloves are pre-broken in now at the factory. Consider that a sign of ill times.

Education is how we rescue tens of millions of teetering Millennial males from the precipice of ironic fedoras and selfie-sticks. This is not a bro-culture thing. Overly obvious and unearned male bonding is born of weakness and homoerotic frat house spankings. Man Rules is a restoration of the male of the species to a gender non-neutral, non-fluid position. All the politically correct movements fail to address the social downsides of exterminating gender distinction. The human species did not arrive at its position of relative dominance by quashing masculine traits. We need male. We need female. This isn't war. It's science.

This book is for you or anyone you know whom needs a swift kick in the testosterone. Not to become arrogant or domineering, but to remember their strong and chivalrous and bold ancestral lines. A growing percentage of the population would like to see male archetypes go the way of the dodo. If you're keeping score, that team is currently winning.

Man Rules are a necessity and somebody had to write them. Ninety-nine rules seemed like a palatable first semester. The journey of a thousand miles begins with a single step. A man understands there are no stops on that thousand-mile journey to use the bathroom.

Lex.

99 MAN RULES

MASCULINITY

Men Are Never the Biggest Pussy in the Room

There is an old joke about two hunters in the woods being chased by a bloodthirsty bear. The dumber one tells the other, "There's no way we can outrun this damn bear. We're going to die". The smarter guy says, "I don't need to outrun the bear. I just need to outrun you." So informs the Theory of Male Relativity. That is, compared to all other men on this planet, you are either more or less manly. You are somewhere in the grand hierarchy between the world's most dominant male and the world's biggest junior boy in a little sailor costume. While your global ranking may not affect your day-to-day, the axiom holds just as much weight in smaller groups of men, like office coworkers, college dorm rooms, beer league softball, and certainly the gathering of underground criminal organizations in the backs of nightclubs.

No matter where a man groups together with other men, it is essential that you not be the weakest male in the room. Every gazelle in the massive herd need not defeat the lion in attack; they just have to do better than the weaker members of their party. What's for dinner? Andy, your happy-go-lucky gazelle cousin. He liked to make daisy necklaces. It's a real shame about Andy. Though less of a shame since you get to live another day. Every group of men has an easy target gazelle. The guy who is the butt of every joke and always has to be the designated driver. If you are unsure who the biggest pussy is in your group of friends, it is likely you.

Regardless of what they believe in Northern New Jersey, not every man has to be an alpha male. Admitting that you are not the toughest man in the world does not make you less of a man, it reveals an honest self-evaluation and a confidence in your place in this world. However, if that same sharp examination indicates you're the most delicate of men, it's time for some self-improvement, or in the very least, a functional disguise. Remember, your goal is to climb the ranks but a little. Do not overcompensate with poor facial hair decisions, steroid ripped muscles, or fantastical tales of high school athletic prowess. That's far too obvious. As is targeting the second weakest, most pathetic guy you can find and insulting his manhood. Other men will see right through this ruse.

Being the biggest pussy is far from a permanent state. You've set the bar so low, it does not take very much to be more of a man. In prison, you might have to beat up the biggest toughest guy in your block to prove your toughness, but in this situation, maybe just take your voice down a couple notes on the scale and stop commenting on how you're dying to see Hamilton.

Men Don't Cry, Especially in the Dark

Men cry at great loss. As in the case of the passing of a loved one or the loss of their football franchise to a Southern state with year-round pleasant weather. When men cry, they know precisely why they're crying, as do the people around them. If you're not sure why you're crying, stop. The same would be true if you were leading police on a high-speed chase at three in the morning or about to board a plane for Syria. If you can't remember what got you to this place, stop. When a man does take the rare opportunity to cry, the appropriate response is to give him space and understand you are witnessing a thrice or so in a lifetime event. Respect the scarcity. Do not touch.

Women cry to express a wide array of feeling quite separate from great loss or obvious tragedy. Women cry while watching movies because women experience a full and rich range of human emotions. Men experience only pain and pleasure, and even then they admit to neither through at least two rounds of waterboarding. Men don't cry in movies any more than they wonder if the real Batman is really dead after being crushed to death by a collapsing building. If you find yourself crying in the dark, check your calendar, as you're probably late for a nail appointment.

The same rule that applies to movies applies to reading a book, attending an art exhibit, or hearing a song on the radio. No crying. The point of any art is to make you feel something and well-constructed art certainly does that. Feeling something is not a reaction you can control. Sharing your feelings certainly is. A man swallows his feelings and buries them deep down in his belly. This occasionally leads to ulcers and heart attacks but at least no one saw you cry. Nobody will ever give you an effeminate nickname for having a myocardial infarction.

When modern women say they wish their men would be more open with their feelings, they're either lying or they're unaware that they're lying.

Women do not want to see men weep. Women are biologically programmed to seek out the strongest member of the tribe. Crying is a sign of weakness. Watch all the afternoon talk shows you want telling you different, they're wrong. Every time Meryl Streep brings a tear to your eye, your girl's legs close another inch.

There are only two exceptions to the crying rule: sports and dead dog movies. Sports movies represent the ultimate in male achievement. When James Caan dies in Brian's Song or Rocky finally beats Apollo Creed, these are moments of masculine exaltation. When Rudy finally gets onto the field, we remember all the times people told us we were weren't good enough and even though they were right, this time, it didn't matter. If you didn't cry when the dog dies, you are a cold heartless bastard. E.T. is close enough to a dog that that's okay too. Also, he didn't really die. Spoiler alert.

Men Don't Discuss Dietary Restrictions

Since the dawn of time, men have eaten whatever the hell they want. Men have consumed everything that can be the least bit digested. Cavemen put anything into their mouths that could fit and a few things that didn't. We grew to be the dominant species on the planet. Men are not as bad as goats, but only because they can kill goats and eat them instead of the garbage the goats eat.

Men aren't picky when it comes to food. Men eat because it is an essential function of survival, not because meals make good excuses to engage in conversation with friends. Men might be chefs who produce food, but they may never be in love with the process of consuming food. If somebody describes themselves as a foodie, you are obliged to politely excuse yourself, exit the room, and never make contact with that individual ever again. Modern men should not live as cavemen. As times have evolved, so have men and their eating habits. A modern man may choose to have a specific diet for various reasons; he just needs to shut up about it. If a man wants to be gluten-free, and dairy free to preserve his bowels, or eat nothing but beef jerky and hot pockets to clog them like apartment pipes, that's his own business.

A man who works for his food is entitled to choose his food as he pleases. However, he may not foist his food preferences upon anyone else. Even a small comment on what other men eat is a major infraction. Are you a registered dietician formally retained to review his dietary plan? You are not. Men don't tell other men how to scratch their nuts, so no man should ever tell another man what to eat. Bodily functions are private, even when performed in public.

A man's diet should never be a burden on another. A man has enough burdens: his job, his mortgage, that ticking time bomb that is his prostate; he doesn't need to worry about what crazy-ass diet another man in his company requires to feel whole.

When even a close friend bitches about your restaurant choice because it doesn't offer any Mediterranean diet options, it's your duty to ask your friend if he wants to see the new tires on your car outside and use this excuse to give him a good roughing up in the alley. Violence is almost never the answer. In the case of men who make a stink about a glycemic index, it is always the answer.

Water Is Not a Precious Commodity

A man has few vices, water isn't one of them. Imbibing water is a necessary function of organic survival. A man treats it thusly, without pomp or circumstance. A man drinks water when he feels thirsty and no whiskey is readily available or it's not yet five o'clock. He doesn't need a water goal or fluid schedule or sixty-four ounces a day to counter the depleting rigor of sitting in an air-conditioned office. If an urologist prescribes a torrent of H20 to flush out the last remnants of an unprotected wild weekend in Las Vegas, follow the advice of your doctor.

A man sips from a fountain after benching his own body weight in sets of six to eight. Take note of the fully hydrated around you. They're not bench-pressing their own body weight. They're complaining about the bathroom wait. In contrast, you peed this morning. You'll pee again tonight. You won't find your next big promotion standing in a restroom line eight times a day.

A man doesn't carry a water bottle around because he understands the difference between the Bedouin desert nomad existence and the universal access to water of the modern Western world. You're not traversing the Gobi; you're making your way across the office park to El Torito for happy hour. It's 800 feet and both your origin and destination have unlimited beverages. If the situation becomes dire, pry the head off of a fire hydrant or even enter a mall. A man might purchase water here and there, but if there's one thing that should chap a man's ass more than paying for parking, it's shelling out cash for a resource that literally falls from the sky.

When a man consumes water he keeps it simple. He doesn't need fruit-infused water or anything containing hibiscus. When a man wants a piece of fruit, he eats a piece of fruit, preferably imported from a war torn nation. A man is not passionate at all about fruit. He's passionate about protecting his home and his family and one day in the future perhaps his planet from alien invaders. Kumquat will never be a key ingredient to defense of the Earth. Water is two hydrogen atoms bonded to one oxygen atom. Keep it that way.

If a man is scouting unknown territories on horseback or is sentenced to a jailhouse road crew for a bar fight protecting a woman's honor, he has the need to transport water with him in an acceptable vessel. Preferably this would come in the form of a green thermos handed down to him from his grandfather who helped to build ships that won a war. Canteens are also acceptable, but they must be coated in felt. A man takes comfort in felt. It reminds him to shave.

Men have enough to worry about without ensuring that their body consists of seventy-eight percent water and never seventy-seven. If a man is still alive that means he's drinking enough water. If the only thing between your halted breath and waning consciousness is a bottle of Evian, have an Evian. You'll live to see another day, but consider you'll live that time as an Evian drinker. Is that really living? A man knows that question is rhetorical.

Men Do Not Fear the Weather

Sometimes it rains. That's a reality we all deal with. But men do not carry umbrellas. Ever. What are you afraid of? Getting wet? Catching the sniffles? It is just water and you're no longer six and being hustled by your mother to shelter. She has maternal instinct and a desire to protect you from harm. You're a man and you can military press your own weight. Do you take waterproof gear with you in the shower?

The same holds for rain boots. If you are afraid of getting your shoes wet, don't wear nice shoes out in the rain. A trench coat is permitted because classic males wore them during the Golden Age of Cinema. Stay away from the cigarettes and fedoras. Not everything classic is classy any longer. If a woman offers to shelter you under her umbrella, you may oblige for the sole purpose of talking her up. That's why she invited you in the first place. She's not a mom and she knows you won't melt.

Men have always had to brave the elements. For the first ten thousand years, no man chided another man to remember to bring his jacket. You brought the coat, or you died, your choice. Talking about the weather was purely ceremonial chatter among men. Your barber mentioned the weather. You mentioned something back in a rote manner. He commenced cutting your hair. There were never any meteorologically significant elements to the interaction.

Our male ancestors marched through waist high snow and waited for hours in the cold and rain to hunt animals for the tribe. Do you think they used an umbrella or rain boots or checked their weather apps to see when they might be able to switch to shorts?

Your grandfather survived torrential tsunamis in a foxhole in WWII while being fired upon and you can't go four blocks without a designer rain blocker over your head like mother's blanket? These innate survivalists sucked it up and held back their shivers, because that's what men do. Women complain about physical discomfort as a means of conversation. Men suffer in silence, to make women aware of their inadequacy.

Men don't wear gloves to keep their hands warm, unless maybe if you are shoveling a driveway full of snow, performing surgery, or climbing Mt. Everest. A man blows on his hands if he's cold. It's almost entirely ineffective, but it's a way to let other men know you're freezing, but you're not a victim. Snow boots are permissible if you are walking through serious snow or ice in situations such as alpine rescue or hunting. You wouldn't expect your mailman to lose a toe in pursuit of his work duties. But if you're using them to get from your front door to your car in the driveway or parking lot, that sound you hear on the wind is the spirit of your great-great-granddad laughing at you.

You can wear a couple of pairs of socks or long underwear if it's less than fifteen degrees. You shouldn't even publicly mention 'the cold' until it's below fifteen degrees. Or hot until it's in triple digits. The same goes for high winds. They're not a tornado. You'd know if they were, because men would be talking about them. Weather that can't kill you isn't worthy of a man's time and consideration. Take a moment to check your drawers and closet for a scarf. Now, give it away to a chilly toddler. You're all grown up.

BODY AND HEALTH

Men Are Toughest in Times of Plague

Men do not get sick. They either get violently ill or insist they're doing fine while in the throes of the black lung. Women get sick, meaning they wear sweatpants and baggy socks and eat soup out of a mug while watching TV. It's more of a light vacation. Men get hopped up on over-the-counter medication and go to work where they insist a dull grey is their natural pallor.

There's no reason why your immune system should be breaking down with any amount of frequency. If you find yourself contracting a virus more than once every few years you're doing something obviously wrong. Like intentionally making out with girls with runny noses or you're teaching preschool. There's no excuse for either. Wash your hands and eat the occasional vegetable. The vast majority of young adults in first world nations should be finding their Tylenol well past expired when they go to look for them.

If you're not a child or a senior, you don't need to go to the doctor for a cold or flu. They're going to tell you to drink a lot of fluids and get some rest. Now you've spent two hundred dollars just to avoid hearing the very same from your mother. There is a time-honored home remedy for a cold called the Two-Hat Cure. Come home from work and hang your hat on the hat rack. Get into bed with a bottle of whiskey, and drink until you see two hats. When you regain consciousness your cold will be gone.

Strongly consider allowing the bug to run its course in your body. In your lifetime there are a finite number of times you can use antibiotics for faster recovery before they cease being effective. Look at your antibodies like American troops. Do not deploy them unless there's an imminent threat to your national security. Stay home and rest, perform the Two Hat Cure, and you'll be ship shape. Showing up to work with a contagious illness is disrespectful to your co-workers. Before you know it the whole company has gone under because you were curious if the glazed donuts in the lunchroom were still moist.

Should your symptoms persist or worsen such that you start feeling extremely remorseful about that kid you bullied in third grade visit your doctor or an urgent care center right away. A man is always searching for the perfect compromise between under-reaction and over-reaction. Like all things in a man's life, you're looking for the sensible middle ground. Guys who confuse toughness with stubbornness end up missing limbs or falling down in elevators. It's a man's job to care for the flock, not merely attend to his own whims. You're no good to anybody else when you're sick. Never visiting a doctor simply makes you selfish. And eventually, you'll find yourself dying from something that was readily preventable, so also stupid. Don't die from stupidity. Your tombstone will be embarrassed next to the real man heroes.

A man's health status is either good to go or seriously ill. "Not feeling so good" is not an option. Don't be the guy who's constantly sensing something coming on or just getting over something. You're not supposed to feel one hundred percent all the time. That's why it's called one hundred percent. Even the nerds in math scored ninety-fives. Now they're billionaire tech pioneers. Ninety-five percent is more than fine. Whatever kills you will never be what you expected. Try to take comfort in that. Those cattle aren't going to drive themselves. Spit your phlegm and saddle up.

There Are No Cosmetics for Men

A man should exercise extreme caution when altering his body. There's a fine line between self-improvement and exterior decorating. Men don't nip and tuck. They cauterize their wounds and live to fight another day. If you're visiting a doctor for purely superficial purposes, you've crossed the line. Does your nose allow you to breathe? Then you don't need a nose job. Break it twice in the ring against the champ and you can file for a special circumstances exception. Your chin doesn't even serve a purpose beyond changing pillowcases. By definition a chin is satisfactory as is. God had a plan for you. It wasn't the perfectly sculpted face. Maybe you'll cure cancer. Nobody inquires as to the looks of the guy who cured cancer.

When it comes to grooming and cosmetic changes, the hard and fast rule is avoid them until your girlfriend threatens to hold out sex. Or in the event your male acquaintances make note of something distasteful about your appearance. Men are genetically programmed not to notice other men's looks unless the situation is alarming enough to represent a danger to the tribe. Not counting that friend who was the only boy among many sisters who can't stand when your collar is out of sorts or your belt doesn't match your shoes. He's still a friend; just don't take him on camping overnights.

If your tooth is chipped to the point of resembling a Himalayan peak, get it capped. If you lose enough teeth that eating corn on the cob is a problem, get implants. That doesn't mean cover your grill in porcelain and start using a toilet brush in the morning. Your new fake teeth should never look more illustrious than your old original teeth. People will notice and silently judge you in a negative light. If you have acne, stop eating crappy food and treat it externally with an over-the-counter product. You don't need a facial. You need two weeks of non-greasy food and ten bucks' worth of Clearasil.

Teeth whitening and use of a tanning bed are unnecessary and potentially dangerous, as one contains harsh chemicals that may cause cancer and the other specifically causes cancer. There's a good chance you've never had cancer. For the sake of argument, assume cancer is worse than not having tanned skin or pearly white teeth. If you're putting your life on the line to look like a male member of a reality TV show cast, that life no longer has meaning.

Manicures and pedicures are positively not for men. Nail clippers you've owned since the ninth grade are. Trim your nails at home while defecating. Both your cuticles and bowels will be proud at your multitasking. There is no reason for a man to enter a salon, which is a French word for extortion. You might lean in to ask your significant other how much longer she might be. If it's an hour, visit the massage parlor next door. Unlike salons, parlors of almost all genres hold wondrous surprises within for men.

Go bald with class. Michael Jordan doesn't lay awake in his bed of spun gold at night thinking about his hair. Plugs make you look like you were assembled from spare parts. Anybody who tells you your fake hair looks great is lying. It's as if you had an ugly baby. I know you didn't know. If you're cursed with a uni-brow, shave a few hairs from the middle and create a definitive divide. The sides are off limits. You don't want to look utterly surprised when your wife tells you she's lost some weight.

Your hair's going to turn grey and you're going to become overweight or underweight because nobody looks like they did in high school after some time. This is why porn casting notices don't encourage ages 35 and over to apply. Let nature take its course. Chicks don't dig guys who obsess over their looks. They dig guys who obsess over the fire pit on their private beach. Don't groom things, build things. Bigfoot doesn't need calf implants and he's your direct competition. Leave this world the way you came in: naked and motivated.

Men Consider Facial Hair Wisely

Should men wear beards? This answer has changed over time and depends on culture and tradition. Some religions demand a man sport chin pubes while others prohibit them. In modern day America, we have the freedom to do whatever we want with our faces. But what kind of facial hair should you grow?

The first question to ask yourself is whether or not you can grow a real beard. You need to be honest with yourself. If a month's worth of growth looks like you shaved the cat and glued patches of matted hair to your face, perhaps you should stay clean-shaven. A full beard is the most acceptable form of facial hair as it is what naturally occurs. All you have to do is not shave. You can shape it for a more sophisticated, commanding look or grow a fuller, longer style like Ernest Hemingway. In the latter case, have a few successful novels under your belt. A Hemingway beard with your first novel "sixty-percent complete" won't do.

What a man never does is grow his beard out in unruly and unkempt fashion. There's a measured but important line between paying inordinate attention to grooming and just being gross. Err on the side that is not gross. You see the unkempt facial hair in hipster districts of major cities. If you are not a lumberjack, a wizard, Santa Claus, or a member of ZZ Top, you cannot allow unchecked growth to be your barber. Sure, cavemen did. They also shit on their feet.

Mustaches are acceptable in very limited specific circumstances. You can sport a 'stache if you are a baseball player, a Middle Eastern dictator, or Tom Selleck. Anyone else will either look like a child molester or a 32-year-old-virgin, or worse, Tom Selleck. If you wear your mustache in a waxed handlebar and aren't in a barbershop quartet, you need more help than one book can provide.

Goatees and soul patches are purely the purview of men who fancy themselves extremely attractive. A man should never fancy himself anything, let alone attractive. Occasionally creepy community college English professors will sport goatees as a means of feigning stature and academic significance. That's even worse than being fancy. Certain Jazz musicians are exempt from this rule, but you're not a Jazz musician. You don't swing, you stand.

The rules of facial hair are complicated enough that the vast majority of men are better off simply shaving. You can never go wrong with a clean-shaven face. It's a sign of cleanliness and basic care that lets other people know you understand basic hygiene, and lets women know there's a decent shot you are STD free.

Venturing into facial hair is a risk with very little upside. No matter how cool you believe it makes you look, divide that by half and then subtract the remainder until you are left with something approximating zero. You once saw a guy with a beard who looked righteous. You probably once saw a man with a cockatoo on his shoulder where it made sense. Live within the rules, not the exceptions. A man saves his energy and risk taking for the important things in life.

Real Men Visit Barbers

Men shouldn't be heavily involved in any grooming process, but you're going to want to get your haircut so you don't look like a slob and you might get a raise. Who a man chooses to cut his hair may well decide which heaven he enters upon his death. Hint, you're going to want to be in the one with John Wayne. The other one blasts EDM music late into the night.

You have two choices in a cut: a barber or a stylist. If you have to wonder if you have enough money to get your hair cut, you're seeing a stylist. If you're getting your hair 'done', you're definitely seeing a stylist. If there's a wall calendar featuring not particularly attractive topless vaguely Latin ladies, you're seeing a barber.

A barber is a crusty gin blossomed guy you race to see when you're hung-over just hours before your buddy's wedding. A barber will ask your name and then pretend you've been coming there for thirty years as he constantly refers to you as Alfred. He doesn't care that you're there because your grandpa told you it's six bucks and his antique barber pole rotates next to a Subway sandwich shop where for another five bucks you can add a sandwich to your recovery morning. A barber will fix you up, tell you a few dirty jokes he's honed over several decades and you'll be on your way. He's never had any complaints or rave reviews. Nobody notices. That's exactly what you want in a haircut. People don't Yelp about chicken nuggets. They're the same chicken nuggets your daddy ate. You know what they are and you know when you need them.

In contrast, a stylist seems perturbed you're overpaying him. He shampoos your hair as if that isn't a personal endeavor. A stylist will ask you how you'd like to look, then sink into a trance and do exactly what he would do to his own hair if he hadn't already mangled it last night while high on poppers. He'll try to hawk some hair product that's emulsified glycerin with the face of a smiling man with brilliant hair brandished on the bottle. It's a trap. You'll never smile like that guy because real men don't smile, they give knowing glances to the Fates while women go down on them for having such practical haircuts and smelling like fire-roasted goat.

Allowing another man to touch your hair rather intimately requires some forethought. Ask yourself what kind of man you really are. Are you the guy who rages in Vegas, sleeps in, and looks really cool eating six-dollar steak and eggs the next morning? Or are you the guy complaining the Circus Circus doubles don't standardly feature a blow dryer? This isn't a haircut. This is your life. Lead it like a man.

Men Do Not Moisturize

There is a reason that Chapstick fits better in a woman's makeup bag than a man's tool belt. It is not a product for men. If a man's mouth is parched, utilizing something that could so easily be confused for lipstick is never an option. Publicly putting anything to your lips the least bit phallus-shaped is never advisable. In fact, eat your damn breakfast banana in the car or the privacy of your own home or office. Nobody wants to see a grown man swallowing a banana. Feel free to write this off as an overreaction as you gurgle your fruit cock.

Some men even go as far as to have a lip moisturizer holder on a lanyard. Using Chapstick is bad enough, but having a permanent place for it is another thing entirely. Secondly, who has a lanyard? Get rid of that thing. It makes you look like a summer camp kid who was too asthmatic for canoeing and had to double up on crafts. The only things you should wear around your neck are ties or, if you are a coach, a whistle.

Applying Chapstick, lip-gloss, lip balm, lotion or any other related products is never acceptable in public. In private, with the bathroom door closed and your family out of the house, you can do what you want. If you think you can complain about your lips being dry, forget it. Men never complain about anything related to wetness or dryness or anything to do with moisture and body parts. You might as well start naming your tears and update your Skype nickname to Hugs'NKisses.

If you've got dry lips it means either you aren't eating enough bacon or you're an arctic explorer. Eat some damn bacon, get back in your igloo, or double down by finding a woman wearing Chapstick and kiss her soundly on the lips with your dried face flesh.

When all else fails, suck it up. It's just chapped lips. Crosscheck the obituaries since forever, nobody's ever died from dry lips. While many a man has passed away from losing his testicles. Ponder that next time you find yourself browsing in the skin and lip care section of the CVS. The condoms are four aisles over. There's no other excuse to be here unless you're picking up something for grandma.

Men Do Not Manscape

Men shave their faces and cut their hair. That is it. The Good Lord made men hairy for a reason. The ladies might vocalize otherwise, but instinctively they want hair on their man's body. Women do not survey the personal ads in search of full body waxed twinks.

There is a feminization of men in this country that can lead to no good, for male or female. The metrosexual vibe was popular several years ago. How long did it last before women realized that they themselves wanted to smell and be groomed and dressed more nicely than their dates?

Body hair arouses a woman because Mother Nature programmed women that way, in the same way men crank their necks and other appendages in the direction of big boobs and a shapely butt. A densely forested body is a sign of fertility and virility. If you shave your chest, back, legs, or crotch you are signaling women that you are devoid of reproductive skills. Your swimmers need floaties. Also, you ruined every razor in the house.

Eyebrows should never be plucked, or waxed. Drag queens and Jersey Shore types shape their eyebrows and unless you want to emulate them you should steer clear of the threading palace. If you happen to be in the small percentage of the population born with a Bert from Sesame Street uni-brow, take care of it quietly and discreetly. Run your razor between your brows when you're shaving your face. Other than that, leave them alone.

Manscaping is decorating your body and men don't decorate. Men put stuff in logical places and leave well enough alone. Men don't do window treatments, they don't buy knick-knacks, and they hate ruffled pillows. The same goes for your body. It is a hairy manly temple. Unless you are a true outlier in the hair growth department, do not desecrate.

The shorn restrictions apply triple for your pubes. Your boys need proper foliage for both aesthetic and health reasons. The hair is there to help keep your sac cool or else your man seed dies off and you might as well too in the anthropological sense. Giving yourself a Brazilian is never an option. It leaves your genitals resembling a baby bird fallen out of a nest, wrinkled on the sidewalk, something no woman would go near. Your sac beard should look like a lush Hassidic and not a stubbly Jake Gyllenhaal. The moment you stop trying to feel pretty is the very moment you start feeling like a man.

Masturbate Like A Spartan

Cleaning the pipes is a reality in a man's life. Masturbation is a chore akin to shoveling the driveway or ruining a romantic comedy with a running barrage of negativity. A man isn't obsessed with tugging his genitals nor does he abhor the process. He performs maintenance straight faced with all the emotion of a line judge. Your penis is designed precisely to make babies. God graced you with making it feel amazing so you would make babies even knowing how much college tuition runs these days.

Under no circumstances does a man pleasure himself. Masturbation is as mechanical as turning a crank or building a makeshift distillery. Do you take pleasure in changing your oil? Maybe just a little, but you certainly don't share your feelings on the subject. The same principle applies to working out at the gym. Your acquaintances don't need to know how awesome it felt, nor do they care. Masturbation is working out your dick. Absolutely nobody needs to know about that.

A man should never consider masturbation as a substitute for sex, the latter far more enjoyable and ultimately determinative of our ability to proceed as a species. A man shouldn't be tuckered out from a long day of browsing the Internet. Imagine you have three or four bullets left and the cavalry with re-supply is several hours away. Don't fire one in the air to drive away the pigeons. If you haven't eaten since a week ago Sunday you're going to tear right into that pot roast. If you drove through In-N-Out right before dinner you're going to sit there and shift around the carrots. Women prefer men of passion. Wild eyed, easily distracted beasts that look like they're about to smash the breadbasket.

A man never employs paraphernalia such as salves, balms, or scented lotions to maintain his reproductive system. Nor does he require complicated visual aids to accomplish his mission. Trust in your ability. Stop lugging around that portable DVD player and an easel. You're blowing your cover.

A man masturbates in the privacy of his own home. If boundaries are not drawn in indelible ink he'll find himself in increasingly undesirable locations such as the smokers' alcove behind office buildings. You don't think everyone at the office knows you just polished your bishop, but they do. Just like your parents knew you'd been drinking when you came home after high school parties. You're glassy eyed and the new girl in Finance just asked to be seated seven more desks away from you. Some devout men go their whole lives without masturbating. You can make it until five o'clock.

Ponytails Are Never the Answer

Ponytails are a hair trap for men. They call them ponytails, because whenever you see one, it is hanging from a horse's ass. They are the absolute single worst hairstyle a man could ever produce or achieve or even be dared into growing.

The ponytail was first introduced in 18th century France, when they called it a "queue" from the French word for tail. There are few things less manly then the French. Their cowardice nearly led to a Nazi victory in World War II. Even now, the men there are so weak; they let their women get away with not shaving their armpits. A man does not allow his woman to be hairy like him. Why not let her borrow your shoes and your car and take your spot in the bowling league? There are lines not to be crossed, the Maginot Line notwithstanding. Armpit hair, ponytails, French things.

It's not just the French who wore ponytails. The hairstyle recently came back into fashion in the 1980s. If there ever was an unmanly decade, it was the 1980s. There are several reasons why a man might choose to have long hair. He might be a rock star, a professional Polynesian athlete, or somebody might be holding his family at gunpoint demanding he grow his hair like a girl.

Unless you fall into one of these categories, there's no excuse for your locks to extend lower than your neck. And if you should ever think about having long hair and tying it up, ask yourself this – isn't everyone related to you going to be begging that kidnapper to take them out? Living with shame is worse than not living at all. Scrunchies is French for eunuch.

Men Do Not Snack

A man eats three meals a day. Breakfast, lunch, and dinner. It never needs to be more complicated than that. It's the trifecta of nourishment. A child may have a snack in between these meals, because they are growing, and have stomachs the size of a coin purse. Hence why you may hear a mother asking after her son or daughter if they had their snack after school or during recess. You're a man. Your stomach can hold an entire pot roast. You don't take recess. You're also not going to grow six inches taller this summer and require shoes two sizes larger. You're no longer eating to grow.

If you're eating between meals it's a sign that you're not eating enough at meals. Or you're overeating. There's no practical reason for either. There are times that a man may find himself in the position to miss a meal such as in the aftermath of an earthquake or when asked to put down an animal by a neighbor who isn't quite as manly. In these instances, you may require a small portion of food, never to be referred to as a snack. The only thing worse than requiring a snack is complaining about being hungry. Women complain about being famished. A man never becomes famished. That's the preeminent sign of a failed hunter. Also women who claim to be starving are lying.

Should you require modest sustenance, your first option should always be nuts. Nuts were invented by God to give a man the protein and calories required to bring home every last steer on the range. There are dozens of kinds of nuts and they all supply the same energy boost without shortening the time between yourself and diabetic boots. Trail mix is not acceptable unless you are hiking with a date and you relish the least tasteful form of fruit. A man doesn't dilute perfectly good nuts with sticky raisins. Raisins are merely shriveled grapes. There's nothing manly about shriveled anything

Sugary treats are tempting for guys who still watch cartoons and play mobile games featuring adorable animals. Temptation is like a man test. If you'd like to score in the top half, skip the candy bar. If you'd like to finish in the top ten percent, dehydrate meat from that mountain lion you speared because it threatened a nearby school. Mountain lion jerky sounds ghastly, but less so than thirteen mauled grade-schoolers. Wild animals are naturally lean; their muscles are packed with protein. You are what you eat. Eat a wild animal.

To a man, snacks are an ancillary item like duvet covers. Avoid them always, and do not speak of them aloud or ever fuss over them in a public setting. A man sits down and eats a proper meal and is done with it. He does not pack diminutive Tupperware containers with precisely allotted non-meals. Is that four ounces of quinoa? If you can answer that question you should place the Tupperware firmly over your nose and mouth and hope you do better at being a man in the next life. Don't forget to burp the seal.

The Gym Is For Maintenance

Through most of human history men had an excess of physical toil and a dearth of food. Staying in physical shape took care of itself. Post-industrial-age man faced the exact opposite problem and built gymnasiums to mimic the toil. A man goes to the gym only so much as he needs to compensate for his sedentary work existence. He doesn't set up residence in the sauna or bring along a deck of cards. He pops in, displaces the equivalent of a Ford F150, and returns to more important activities in life. Working out is a health issue like eating vegetables or punching hipsters who smoke e-cigarettes. It's not a vocation. It's certainly not a lifestyle.

26

MAN RULES

Men don't take classes at the gym. Classes are for children and those struggling to learn English. A man doesn't spin, he does bench-presses with negligible form to prove a point to the guy with the mullet who showed him how to do it right six years ago. Pilates are for people who can't change a tire. Aerobics are extremely healthy but if you're in a brightly lit room with EDM blaring, you've got to question the worth of extending your life given how you're choosing to live it.

A man doesn't wear Lycra tights or bodysuits unless he's squeezing into a bank vault. He's suspicious of anything that grips his testicles unless he's planning to screw it later. A man wears a crusty T-shirt at the gym because he's not there to impress anybody nor does he delight in doing laundry. He doesn't stand around talking about last night's Bachelor or discuss the intricacies of Nietzsche with his spotting partner. A man needs no spotter because he's ultimately confident in his strength and ability to sustain injury. Talk sports or keep silent.

While lifting weights, a man doesn't grunt or scream aloud. That's reserved for women who are baring children or filming erotica. Men suffer in silence. They make only the slightest puff of exhalation, even as their anuses prolapse during a squat-thrust. Swallow your physical pain as your ancestors have done for eons.

If you're not sweating, you're not working out. However, a man doesn't shower at the gym after he works out unless it's a scheduling must. You should clean yourself in a public setting as a purely voluntary matter. When showering it's appropriate to practically address the imperfect hygiene of the male of the species. Don't announce it and certainly don't make a public fuss, but be aware there is fungus and sperm on that shower floor. Wear sandals. After the shower, put on a towel that neither conceals or explicitly reveals your manhood. A man has nothing to hide nor is he putting anything out there, much like an aggressive monk with a pill problem. Men who revel in nudity in the gym locker room are under a decidedly false impression of their own masculinity. You might shave naked at home. This isn't your home. Don't shit with the door open and cover up your genitalia. A man who walks around naked isn't showing you his abundance of muscles, he's showing you that being naked in front of other men is thrilling for him. Make of that what you will as you choose hunting trip cabin-mates.

The gym is not a bar or a club or your local hangout. It's a service station. Fill your tank, change your oil and move on. If you're detailing, you're doing too much. Men don't make themselves pretty because pretty won't save your life in a leopard attack. They make themselves just strong enough to make the leopard think twice.

Sunscreen Is an Excellent Form of Protection… for Women and Children

The sun is 92 million miles away. You shouldn't be afraid of it. Men have worked in the sun for centuries without so much as a single SPF of protection.

Sunscreen wasn't even invented until the 1940s. That means that every man who lived before 1940 lived without sunscreen. Cowboys spent all day in the hot sun and never once stopped to lather themselves in Banana Boat. The only protection their skin needed was sweat and dirt and that's all you should need too. You are not a cowboy, but you should try to emulate one.

Women should wear sunscreen because they are elegant creatures and their beauty must be protected. Children should wear sunscreen because they are weak and their underdeveloped body cannot handle the sun. But a man has no excuse. So, if you see any other man rubbing on sunblock in public, it is your duty as a man to smile at him knowingly with your naturally tanned skin. You both know very few women are deeply attracted to men with the pallor of fine china. George Hamilton got a lot more action than Edward Scissorhands.

If you never use sunscreen again, you might get burned once or twice. But a little sunburn never killed anyone. Except for those it did. Consult your family tree. Most likely it'll peel, and new, tougher skin will grow in its place. Your old weak pale skin will become stronger darker skin. Sunburn may hurt a bit, but remember that pain is merely weakness leaving the body. So next time you have radiation burns from the Mother Sun, just relish in the pain. That is the pain of becoming a real man.

Men Tattoo Responsibly

Tattoos have the potential to be manly. As is any practice that involves pain, blood, and needles in an entirely voluntary manner. Your grandfather might have gotten a bloody knife tattoo in Okinawa after banging four hookers and killing a platoon of enemies with a tree branch. That's an awesome tattoo. Less awesome is tattooing a girl's name on your neck.

It doesn't matter if she is the mother of your children and your wife of fifteen years or a girl you've slept with twice at her apartment while her roommate was watching Showtime, when you tattoo a woman's name to your body you are effectively ending the relationship. One never knows what tomorrow will bring and even a happy marriage can end quicker than you can say, "I caught my wife banging that actor wannabe who works at the Coffee Bean". You are tempting The Fates when you tattoo a girl's name on your body. Many a man has made the walk of shame to the laser removal center for the costly and painful erasure of a former lover.

As go women so go sports teams. No matter how much you love your local sports team or their current QB, don't get sports teams or player's numbers tattooed onto any part of your anatomy. If you think small lettering on your calves don't count, then you're of the belief that perhaps just singing one show tune a day doesn't count against your masculinity score either. What if your hero is traded to a rival team? What if he is caught doping, is arrested for kiddy fiddling, puts on dogfights, or murders his wife? Tattoos are permanent; free agency is not.

You must avoid any tattoos related to routine accomplishments. You graduated from McKinley High? Congratulations. So did the dude that work nights frying nuggets at McDonalds and Homeless Pete out behind the liquor store reminding you how his doctor insists Thunderbird is the only way to save his heart. The same tattoo rule applies to college attended. Ask yourself this: is this as far as I'm climbing in this life? If you're the NCAA championship quarterback on campus, perhaps so. Otherwise, hopefully graduation really is a stepping-stone for you to something better. If you want to show school pride you can donate to the booster club, cheer on the team at games, or buy a fifteen-dollar sweatshirt for fifty dollars. You're now proudly one of 500,000 living alumni of The Ohio State University. That club isn't exclusive enough for sub-dermal permanent marker.

A man should never tattoo a Chinese or Japanese symbol on his body if he isn't Chinese or Japanese. And, no, a semester abroad doesn't count. Maybe the Peace Corps in your third year of overseas service. There is no greater visual tell of being a follower than having an Asian symbol tattoo visible on your body. As a gaijin from the suburbs, chances are you can't read Japanese script. How do you know that it really means "Good Fortune" or "Warrior"? It could mean "Asswipe" or "Micro-Penis" and you would entirely deserve such a fate. The same rule applies for any "tribal" or cultural tattoo that doesn't belong to your heritage. You are merely romanticizing a culture different from your own for the sole purpose of bringing yourself attention. That's not racist, just lame. Stick to anchors, skulls, or knives. But earn them first.

As with other things about a man, size matters. A tattoo should fill almost to completion the area it inhabits. Don't want to fill your whole shoulder? Afraid it will be visible at work? A tattoo isn't for you. Fulfill your rebel heart some other way. If your tattoo is smaller than a quarter, you should have skipped it and wrecked a motorcycle instead.

THE OPPOSITE SEX

On Meeting Women

When approaching a woman who fascinates some portion of your being, consider this daunting truth: you have three seconds to make a first impression. She'll either cringe or speak of that moment fondly to your grandchildren a thousand rounds of sex down the road. Women know the situation is delicate and you're basically trying to defuse a ticking time bomb using nothing but a gum wrapper and lint. And they're trying to sabotage it. This isn't done out of pure amusement. They're sizing you up. If you can't maneuver your way through an awkward conversation full of half-truths how are you going to fix the garbage disposal? It's evolution. Trust that she doesn't need your specific penis to fulfill her destiny.

Whatever bar, club, disco, speakeasy, hookah lounge or artisanal moonshine distillery you find yourself in, follow the same basic protocol. Confidence is key. If you don't have it, fake it. Pretend you stopped at the local gymnasium to set the military press record, or that you just got promoted or that your car starts. Project this virtual testosterone inward. A man doesn't brag, he just looks like he could do a good job of it. Getting sloppy drunk and spinning spittle filled tales of glory day stories isn't a substitute for anything other than winding up lonely.

The universe plays cruel tricks, and none is more paradoxical than the following axiom: act like you care the least about what you care the most about. Women can smell desperation. The more you're evening, week, or lifetime depends on this consummation between man and woman, the less chance it's going to happen. That's how life works. It's why the down on his luck gambler perpetually loses on double aces. Women are programmed to land the guy with the best genes in the Waffle House. The superior mate is inherently rife with options. Pull off that illusion and you've turned the tables.

Avoid hackneyed pickup lines or coming off rehearsed. If sounding natural doesn't come naturally to you, a simple hello is usually your best option. If a lady has been harassed through the evening by the nearby celebrating rugby team and has her guard up, a random non sequitur will distinguish you nicely. Who's your favorite figure skater? She wasn't expecting that. Now she can drop the bored drink stirring routine and admit she's randy. If you're in a group setting, try a friendly wager. My idiot friend here just bet me I wouldn't come talk to you. The joke is on him, you have no morals.

The entire mating endeavor is purely a numbers game. People who claim to have found the perfect person as some beginner's Kismet are almost certainly lying. The more you step up to the plate, the more you connect, even if you're hit rate is horrible. This is not an endorsement of any type of rapid fire, pick-up artist routine. You need only visit one of those hotel seminars and scan the room to understand why you don't want to be part of that frustrated mob. Open yourself up to meeting women everywhere you go. Beyond bars, try places you know attractive women frequent. Bookstores with puns for names, over-priced organic produce stores, and arts and framing stores. If she asks you why you're there, just laugh and say, "I should be asking you the same question." You shouldn't be, but she won't follow up.

Your ancestors used to have to hunt and gather and labor for every single necessity in life. You're down to one. Women. Make an effort. Treat her like she's special. If you could live out your days with only your dog, you'd be doing so already.

Dating Is Complicated, Keep It Simple

Meeting unknown members of the opposite sex was never meant to be pleasant or comfortable, merely a necessary process to keep the species viable. Spending one-on-one time with a total stranger while suppressing any indication of your desire to have sex with them is necessarily awkward. Any association with the word "date" should be avoided as it conjures up images of overdressed people stiffly boring the hell out of each other. When you meet a woman who tickles your fancy, invite her to 'hang out' or 'grab a drink.' This is the first of numerous inquiries leading eventually to a marriage proposal. Don't blow your once-in-a-lifetime use of poetry and Old English asking her out for the first time.

Ideally, you come across as polite, but leave her not completely confident that you'll even show up. Ten years from now you will be lying when you say you remember your first date with her. She will remember everything in as great as detail as you do that time your dad introduced you to your sports hero. Set the tone early. You're kind and you're nice, but you're also a man with options. If this isn't actually true, fake it.

For your first "hang out", do not complicate an already delicate situation with extraneous activities such as parasailing or fashioning pottery. If you've turned to GQ for great first date ideas that will blow her away, you've already lost and you should consider the clergy. Find a classy but not expensive bar in proximity to some body of water natural or manmade and order a couple drinks. Some men will turn to their local coffee house as the ideal place to casually meet up one-on-one with a woman of interest. Don't. Latte is French for estrogen. Starbucks meet-ups immediately put you in the friend category. You don't need more friends, not even amazing new friends with vaginas. You need to find a sexually liberated good woman and get on with your life.

Whoever came up with the idea of going to the movie theater, as a dating activity most likely died a virgin. Sitting next to someone you don't know for two hours in an environment where you're unable to verbally communicate is a cruel predicament. In the old days when teen girls were under strict societal rules about sexual behavior, the dark movie theater was a place where you could make out and feel up the female love of your life. It served a purpose. Nobody's getting to second base anymore in shopping mall Cineplexes. Take your grandfather to a movie. He'd probably appreciate it and you two have already said everything there is to say.

After the first date, it's all about what comes next. She's agreed to see you again which means you passed the test. Don't crow, it was probably a C.

While she'll remember your first date forever, it's actually the second date that will seal your coupling fate. Invite her to do something where you can nonchalantly display your mastery of some subject. Trying something brand new is a lousy idea and you'll look like an ass. Women aren't attracted to guys who are bad at things. Spending the day falling off a stand-up paddleboard is hardly impressive. Sporting events work, but not ideal nor do they earn you any measure of uniqueness. "I met this great guy and he understands the rules of hockey," isn't something any girl ever has gushed about to her roommates. Not outside of Minnesota.

Dinner is never a good venue for the first several dates. You're a man. You eat like a man. Your mother yelled at you at the dinner table because etiquette doesn't come naturally to you. She didn't understand. Neither will your date. You were built for moving couches. You don't do mealtime well. It's uncomfortable to be stared at while shoving meatballs into your face. You can't take her to your local dive for cheap eats so the date instantly becomes expensive. That creates tension.

Even if she spends the entire meal talking about how her cat is super nuts when ovulating, you most certainly will be expected to pay, and you should. If food becomes politely necessary, take her to that secret spot tucked away next to the long ago burned down warehouse that makes insane little something or others. It's a great icebreaker, the food will be priced right, and you'll come off looking like a knowledgeable local. Even if you just blew into town a week ago, you're going to want to look like a knowledgeable local. Google is a pre-date must.

When the evening starts winding down to its natural conclusion, let the situation breathe. Don't invite her back to your place or say anything suggestive until you're reasonably sure it will work. And not because you believe you're irresistible. You're not. She needed a date. You had the leverage. You need sex. She has the leverage. Treat this like Roosevelt treated Yalta. Put some sober thought into how best to proceed. You can never ever take back, "So, you wanna get it on?"

Barring religious proclamations, if you haven't had some kind of intimate contact by the third date it's time to move on. Women decide if they're going to sleep with a man within minutes of meeting him. She already knows the answer. If she's drawing it out it's not because it's a hot yes. You're now officially wasting her time and your time by bowing to politeness and not agreeing to be friends who never ever see one another again. You shouldn't fall in love with the first woman you sleep with nor should you fall in love with a woman who won't sleep with you. Find the happy middle.

When she informs you her roommate is out of town for the weekend, you'll know the middle is upon you. Use a condom. This entire rule could've been summed up with just those three words. You can easily put failed dates out of your mind. Babies and STDs much less so.

Online Dating Is Surrender

There's a time in every man's life when he feels the weight of loneliness tug upon his soul. The degree to which the desire for companionship precisely mirrors the need for sexual intercourse is a matter for science. The heart wants what the heart wants. The brain invents a myth to make that raw passion more magical than unseemly. Fortunately, there are establishments that serve you liquor to the point that getting naked with a complete stranger seems kosher. For those seeking more sober mixers with the opposite sex, the office, gym, bookstores, and farmers markets provide a socially acceptable playground for flirting and courting. Your den by way of a Cat-5 cable isn't an appropriate place to meet a woman. Your parents didn't meet because your dad upgraded his profile. They met because dad got his ass out of his apartment and into the field. The same goes for boar hunting.

Online dating may seem alluring. Multibillion-dollar service industries aren't built on uninspired business plans. But there are no shortcuts in nature. Quality women aren't attracted to men who toil on their computers humble bragging about their hair transplants and pretending they love art exhibits. Women want men who get things done. It's always tempting to order a Papa John's and wave the white flag, but you don't think about processed cheese when you're chatting up that hot blonde who smells like strawberry car freshener.

For every man in your position there's a woman refreshing her inbox to see if that Persian hiking enthusiast wants to confirm a tenuous coffee date next Arbor Day. Eventually she will get frustrated and head out of the house to make some bad decisions. Be prepared. Pour yourself one stiff drink and get in the zone. The only trait every single man on this planet shares in common is the desire to plunge his penis into something warm and moist. There is going to be competition. It's like Best Buy on Black Friday morning. This isn't the year you'll be the only one who remembered.

MAN RULES

When in view of any member of the opposite sex, stop playing with your phone. Women know you're texting yourself frittata recipes and not ordering hits on spies as your posture suggests. Imagine checking your phone is akin to tossing your hair and re-applying your lipstick and you'll have a clearer understanding of how you appear to your future potential ex-wife.

Despite all the hurdles of online dating, you may find yourself dabbling on Tinder as a silly pastime on par with fantasy golf. Take into consideration that it's far easier for a woman to meet men offline than it is for a man. A reasonably attractive woman will be hit on by no less than four men while simply running into the store for tampons. At least ten will show her the proper way to perform arm curls at the gym. If she's in a short skirt or tight pants, that number rises exponentially. A man can enter a store or gym countless time during his lifetime and never once be asked for his phone number by a woman hoping to get into his pants.

Given the disproportionality, consider in general what kind of women might require online channels for finding potential mates. There might be a few abnormalities. Their photos will all be snapshots from Google Earth with a Vaseline filter and they'll have enough skeletons in their closet to rival Jeffrey Dahmer. Not all, but most. In person courting tends to catch most of these obvious warning signs that are completely lost online. The truly dark elements won't be revealed until after the "I do's".

Understand that everyone you know will eventually review you're online dating activity and mock you relentlessly. Everybody is jealous of their friend who meets girls every time you go out. Nobody is jealous of their friend who brags about all the women he's connecting with through his eHarmony profile. Don't make it easy on them. Lay off the sexual innuendos and never ever share naked photos. Your grandfather didn't develop semiconductors and integrated circuits for MIT so you could grow up to snap selfies of your junk and transmit it to a woman you've never met and may even have a bigger cock than you. One of your dick pic recipients will almost certainly be a friend of your former receptionist and before you know it your name is now the punch line to a joke being told across eighty-percent of your LinkedIn connections.

Consider honesty in your profile. If you end up rendezvousing with the extremely rare basement-dwelling super model you want her to be slightly disappointed, not crestfallen. Don't come in a foot under and fifty pounds over listed height and weight. Don't lie about your station in life or resources at your disposal. Shine a positive light on what you do have. Dating isn't an airport gift shop where people buy overpriced crappy mementos to relieve their boredom. A good woman will respect your trend line more than your current standings. Show her you're on the move. You're ambitious and dedicated and you love children. That last part may be the one exception to the honesty is the best dating policy rule. Women inherently prefer men who pretend to like children versus those who won't even make the effort to pretend.

Online dating should be considered a last resort. Somewhere just below allowing an aunt to set you up with her friend's daughter and just above putting a .22 slug into your forebrain. Every minute you spend left swiping ringer profiles on Tinder could be spent relaying tales of that one summer in

Ibiza to women in the analog world. Every dollar you spend on a Premium Membership could go towards buying dinner and drinks for a cute-looking Midwestern girl in town for a multi-level marketing conference. For all the promoted statistics about happy end results from online dating, search your soul. You know it's simply not true. Put some elbow grease into this campaign. There are few things that come for free in this life. A memorable sexual relationship is not one of them.

Men Do Not Ignore Warning Signs in Women

Ninety percent of women make perfectly fine girlfriends. There's a solid chance you're dabbling in the other ten percent. Men climb mountains because they're there. The wrong girl is always there. Instinct is a double-edged sword with both the power to sustain your success and the potential to cause your demise.

When seeking out a female mate for an intimate relationship, keep an open mind. Whoever you assume might be a great match will inevitably turn out to be a failed venture and vice-versa. This isn't like predicting who's going to make the NBA Finals. There are only ever five or six teams that have a shot. This is like using science to assess the Lotto numbers. How many mathematicians do you see hoisting those giant cardboard checks?

Do not confuse open-mindedness in meeting women with anything suggesting reckless behavior. Invariably all failed dating relationships can be traced back to completely missed signs and clues from the initial stages of a relationship, like a series of "Warning! Bridge Out!" road signs a man breezes past while looking to win favor with his reproductive parts. There are recurring red flags that a man should look for when considering courting a woman. Consider these ten obvious but often overlooked deal breakers and you'll actively reduce your future alimony payments by at least half.

Has She Ever Worked in the Sex for Pay Industry? Prostitutes, strippers, and porn stars do not make for the type of woman you want to settle down with, or even leave unattended in you home near anything that will fit inside a clutch. Even if this occupation is in her past, you must consider it as currently relevant. Many men have tried and failed. Choose to ignore this work history entry and you'll have the cops at your house once a week and a lawyer on retainer.

Is She Rude to the Waitress? The natural inclination of humans is to feel sorry for people who menially serve others. That's why the tipping system was invented. It's a means of displacing guilt. If you're dating a girl who is snarly with the help, this means she's dead inside. If she's nice to you, it's because she wants something. It could be money or status or she could just be lonely and aware that she's largely disliked at work. Just know she stares at you while you're sleeping while grasping scissors.

Does She Have the Voice of a Small Child? Even very petite women don't naturally sound like little girls. It's an affectation. This can be mildly cute at first until you realize it's because her uncle lived next door while out on parole. It then becomes exceptionally grating. When she asks to pass the salt it sounds like a cry for help. She does need help. But not the kind you're trained to give

<u>Does She Lie?</u> Even if you catch a small fib, lose her number. She claims to be a vegetarian and orders the chicken sliders. She'll start small and work her way up to a bogus cancer diagnosis to keep you from attending bachelor parties. It's not the dishonesty that kills you. It's the fact she thinks you're too dull to notice. That doesn't bode well for your future happiness.

<u>Does She Have Poor Hygiene?</u> The nature of long-term relationships is that both parties tend to care less over time. It's important to start from a place of hyper-caring so the descent won't be as deep. If a woman is not ship-shape and smelling something wonderful early on, you're looking at future years of Longshoreman scent. You should be clean as a whistle yourself, but she already knows to look for this because women were born with at least half the information in this book.

<u>Does She Seem Desperate for Attachment?</u> If she's discussing moving in after the second date or needs help tying her shoes, something is amiss. She will soon be calling you on your lunch break and insisting you call her pet names in front of your co-workers. Next comes the desire to make-out during the last two minutes of the 4th quarter of Game 7, because sports aren't as important as your feelings for one another. She means well but it's simply too much to deal with. Buy her a tabby cat on your way out the door. You'll both look back some day very thankful for this tradeoff.

<u>Is She Big on Free Stuff?</u> After an initial few dates a woman should offer to split the bill. Naturally, you don't allow her to pay. It's a silly dance but still a reflection of character. If she explicitly asks you to buy her some shoes or a purse, disappear mid conversation, leaving a you-shaped puff of smoke. She

uses guys. Don't be that sap. Prostitution is an honest profession compared to what she has in store for you. You can do better.

Does She Express Disapproval of Your Friends? Your friends aren't Nobel scientists, but it's up to you to make the call on their character. If she gives you a hard time about your friend who's a ladies' man or about you going to your buddy's place for the game, it means she intends to alter every aspect of your life. You'll soon be sporting a blazer to the tennis match on Paintball Sunday. She thinks she's better than you and perhaps she's right. Contemplate that evaluation while single.

Has She Made Any Effort to Be Famous? Do you notice that she seeks out public attention, or worse yet, continually mentions how her life should be a reality show? Everybody wants to be a star at eight. If she's in her twenties thinking about nothing but being on camera, point to the horizon and run away while she's fallen for your ruse. Any mention of involvement in the reality show industry means she has sociopathic tendencies and will end up hacking into your bank account out of sheer boredom and an implicit need to spread chaos. Break up with her, she'll take it much easier now than she will on the season finale.

Is She Still Close with An Ex-Boyfriend? You promised your last girlfriend you'd remain friends, but you knew that was just a hedge against a lonely night before you found your next. Women break up with men when they can stand them no longer. If her ex-boyfriend is in her life in any way, either they're still doing it or he still wants to and she's leveraging that to get airport rides. It's a sign of disrespect. Before you know it you're buying panties to leave around the house to get even and quizzing her on their former sex life. Just ruin this dinner before the trouble of making it.

These are not the full extent of the warning signs, but like the bible that contains 613 commandments, the top ten really are the ones affecting your final grade.

Men Don't Carry On Romantic Relationships Casually

Every woman you meet will either be somebody you know for the next couple of minutes or commit to a life together for the next fifty years. Since you have no reasonable way to predict the future, you must advance with some intelligence about your interactions from the beginning. The start of a relationship is akin to the first round of a lightweight boxing match. There's a healthy amount of dancing and feeling out. Going for broke only makes you appear desperate. It also opens your ribs up for punishing body shots.

A man is never clingy with the girl he's seeing. There's no excuse to drape your arm around a woman's neck. You're entering California Pizza Kitchen for an early dinner, not Bartertown looking to snake a quart of fuel. It's been many years since you could claim a woman simply by manhandling her. She either likes you or she doesn't. Reminding the world that you're insecure about your masculinity won't help the cause. By the same token, don't allow her to grasp onto you in social situations like she's on the sinking Titanic. It's a tacit relinquishment of your right not to be treated like a stuffed animal. Spooning is for after-sex. If you provide close body contact like a cheap affection whore, there will be less and less frequent after-sex moments.

Public affection is fine to a degree. A few kisses here and there in front of others remind her that she's special. Showing obvious affection in front of her girlfriends is especially critical because secretly she wants nothing more than to be happier than all of her friends combined. Don't be put out by having to occasionally nuzzle the woman who may bear your children one day, thus relieving you of all future nuzzling. You probably already go much farther daily with your dog.

While pecks and hugs are the duty of a boyfriend, don't be that disgusting couple dry humping on the salad bar. Prove yourself in the bedroom, not in front of the guys from your softball team. Correspond daily but do not engaged in incessant texting and phone calls. She doesn't need running hole-by-hole updates of your putt putt skins game. Don't set the precedent for nightly chat sessions about her friend's silly cats. You're her man, not her best friend. Understand that you can never be sufficient at the latter or will only create disappointment down the road.

Early stage couples presume they are tied together like a three-legged race. It's important to remember you both had lives prior to meeting. Yours mostly entailed drinking Schlitz and familiarizing yourself with the intricacies of the pornography business, but it was a life nonetheless. You don't have to attend culturally uplifting functions with her. She need not don a ball gown and tag along to the fantasy baseball draft in the bowels of Hooters. Draw a line in the sand.

Lay out as a clear example that if you want to hit up a toga party with your buddies on the eve of Valentine's Day, she may not be invited. You don't need to see each other every day. You simply don't have that many cool stories. And if you're doing it to get laid more often, she will catch on quickly and decide you need a period of celibacy to get to know each other better. Try to remember that women are innately smarter than you at managing the opposite sex.

Eventually her birthday will come around. Because the universe needs a good laugh, this always happens a few weeks into the relationship when you're not quite sure what your role is. Treat it like Secret Santa at the office. Pick out a well thought-out yet monetarily modest gift such as those cool headphones she mentioned. Understand that crotch-less panties would be for you but not entirely practical for her. She needs to know you care. You need her to know fifty bucks is your max limit on gifts. This is all about setting expectations. The lower the bar the simpler the hurdle.

If you like a girl, lock it up. Tell her the relationship is exclusive and get it over with. That's what having a girlfriend means. You've spent enough time at the bar. They can take down your Christmas stocking. Adjust the settings on your phone. Who's Ashley? My hardwood floor guy. She's not stupid.

You don't have to have a girlfriend. Your father is not the Duke of anything and you don't have obligations to the kingdom. This is an entirely voluntary decision. Be the lone wolf if you please. Many men are suited to the bachelor lifestyle. Be honest with yourself. Don't get into relationships with women just to try and get out of them. Lying and deceiving is not the business of a man. Nor is hurting women through a lack of forthrightness. Some day your balls will be old and wrinkled. Let them feel like they did good.

So You Knocked Her Up

Producing and caring for children is an invaluable aspect of the human experience. The bond a man feels between himself and his offspring is indescribable. The joy cannot be matched by anything else in the universe. That's assuming you did it on purpose. Otherwise that little larva can ruin your life.

Unexpected pregnancies happen. You get intoxicated and forget to use a condom. You remember to use a condom but forget how. That stripper Google Earthed your home address and deemed you her ticket out of the Spearmint Rhino. Accidents can happen at surprisingly opportune times for your partner.

If you and your girlfriend or wife planned on having kids a bit down the road and you've got a steady job and some prospects for better, roll with it. You've saved yourself a lot of emotionless obligatory sex in the name of conceiving, the regimented nature of which will damper your passion to the point that sex is as exciting as a tooth brushing.

Sometimes, for a variety of reasons, it's just not the right time. Maybe you just got laid off or you're on your way to build Ebola triage huts for a year in the Ivory Coast. Sometimes it's not the right woman. Maybe you knocked up your masseuse or your cousin who seemed far too attractive to be in your family, but she is. There is an option. Abortion. It's neither neat nor tidy or to be taken lightly. But neither are joint visitations at your baby mama's halfway house.

If you have reservations about this decision, you can't be the one to carry the day. Understand that the pregnant party in this transaction has a biologically and emotionally greater interest than you. You're operating here as a minority partner. Act accordingly.

Assure your partner that you're open to making a beautiful, well cared-for baby in the future. She has a thing growing inside of her, and does not instinctively want to part with it. She might not be thinking clearly. It's up to you to steer her in the right direction. You could be living on a catamaran in Key West nine months from now. It wouldn't be fair to the kid.

A decent man will accompany his pregnant partner to the clinic, pay, sit, and wait. No matter how much you want to believe this is a shared culpability, that's not how men operate in relation to women. She doesn't have to carry half the furniture when you move. You're the man. This was your fault. Take time off work and be there for support. If you need to drive across godforsaken parts of Texas, don't think, do it. It's a few days or eighteen years. As a practical matter, if she thinks you don't care, she's more inclined to keep the baby. Spite babies end up stealing your hubcaps down the road.

Learn from this episode and don't repeat the mistake. Use protection. Drink less often. Be aware of the energy you're putting out there. You're not an NFL cornerback. It's not amusing to litter the annals of illegitimacy with your born and unborn children. These are the types of milestones in your life that live with you forever. Men don't have time for regrets. Create as few as possible.

A Man Puts Some Time Into Gifts For His Woman

Modern feminism prefers to intentionally ignore the past million years of evolution. That and women deciding not to shave are its two greatest offenses. Men and women respond to similar events in distinct manners. Not all men, not all women, but, by and large. Plus, you don't have time to learn all the exceptions to the rules, just the rules, hence this book.

Men may appreciate a token of appreciation on their birthdays yet they don't base their self worth for the next orbit around the sun on the necktie's thematic relevance to their life. A man may look forward to the holiday season yet he doesn't start shopping for his second cousin the moment he returns from the neighborhood Halloween party. Men need to be left alone. Women need to feel special. You must pretend gift-giving occasions for others matter more to you than what you have recorded on your DVR for when you get home.

You need to get your girlfriend something nice. "It's the thought that counts" is an expression coined by a man who won't be getting any tonight. It's a lot of pressure, but so is carrying a baby to term for nine months inside your belly, and you don't have to ever do that. A hundred years ago men your age died from the flu. You need to spend an hour four times a year procuring a decent gift for a woman who actually tolerates seeing you naked.

Do yourself a favor and shop early. Ideally just ask her what she wants, see if it's available on Amazon, and be done with the entire arduous process. Female characters in movies appreciate the value of surprise. In real life women appreciate getting exactly what they want. Through no fault of your own, you can't give her that, but do your best to approximate.

Should you find yourself scrambling at the mall an hour before her birthday party it's going to be obvious. Those mukluks could fit Shaquille O'Neal. Also, you live in a desert. Avoid shoes. Your lack of research will be glaring. You may attempt a garment as a gift but enter the octagon knowing she'll almost certainly return what you purchased. Which is precisely why you have to spend more money than would make sense to a man. Once the cashier informs her you pulled it off the clearance rack you're in for major problems. This is why clearing the gift beforehand works exceedingly well.

Refrain from anything cooking or cleaning related. She will twist this into you demanding she leave the party to scrub the toilet and make you a sandwich. Which would be nice, but it is her birthday. Likewise, completely omit from your shopping list anything explicitly sexual such as lingerie or intimate toys or costumes of any kind. This will be met with the accusation that you see her purely as an object to satisfy your carnal desires and do not appreciate her questions regarding the rules of college football. She shops or thinks about shopping every day of her life. Leave the decisions to go naughty up to her. Gag gifts don't work either. It just shows you're not taking this whole thing seriously when your entire goal is to pretend otherwise.

Most people in modern America have everything they need and a garage full of stuff they don't. There's a huge business in personal storage unit rentals based on the fact we're overflowing with unnecessary crap. If you can locate a hard-to-find specialty item she's mentioned but has been unable to lay hands on, your effort will be repaid through new sex positions and the forgiveness of your drunken antics. Think about a replacement crank for her old record player. An antique snow globe exactly like the one her grandfather gave her but you broke when moving. When in doubt, simply splurge. Denying evolution means denying that women are attracted to and appreciative of men who are good providers. She can get emotional warm and fuzzies from her friends and manicurist. Build her a nice nest.

Men Make Clean Breaks

A man either fights to keep relationships together or he cleaves them asunder. There is no halfsies in a union involving a man and a woman. Gray is the color of failure.

At some point you will be in a position to dump a girlfriend. It's not fun or pleasant but sometimes for the greater good it simply has to be done. Man up. If you no longer want to be with a girl, you are doing both you and her a favor by breaking it off swiftly and cleanly. Be honest, direct, and unambiguous. Don't insist you want to stay friends, that you may get together in the future, or that you'll call her often down the road. When you break up with someone you are stating clearly, "I don't want to see you ever again. Ever. Really." Don't put it this way (unless she slept with your brother, or sold your car for heroin), but make damn sure this is the sentiment.

MAN RULES

Do not return for comfort sex. There are billions of women on the face of this planet. Your former girlfriend is the single worst person for you to engage sexually.

There are men out there who don't want to be the bad guy or be put in a position to hurt a woman's feelings When you aren't honest or forthright, you are ultimately going to cause the girl more pain in the long run. Sometimes in life men have to do crappy things, and breaking a girl's heart is one of them. Put on your big boy pants and send her packing.

Do it in person. Only a coward breaks up via text, email, or even phone. Stand before your girlfriend and state clearly and succinctly, "It's been great but I don't want to see you anymore. Here's your toothbrush, your hairdryer, and your birth control pills". Change your locks, un-friend her on Facebook, and move on with your life. As much as your grandmother has told you otherwise, you're not all that unique or awesome. She will survive without you.

Beyond hurt feelings, it's important to be direct to prevent "girl who won't go away" syndrome. Millions of men believing they are softening the blow have had their breakups blow up in their face when their girlfriend can't take a hint. Or she doesn't want to. She'll show up on your doorstep when you begin dating other women, try to have sex with your fantasy football commissioner, and slash your tires. Eventually your co-workers will be staring at you like a murderer in their midst as a crazy woman yelling your name is being escorted from the building by security.

Immature men are fond of declaring how their girlfriend or former girlfriend is crazy. Mature men understand their role in this disaster going back to the moment of first coupling down to the inability to break cleanly from the relationship. There is a clear correlation between mentally unstable girlfriends and men too weak to be direct. Don't be that man. A man wants his pets to live.

Pretend to Love Her Friends

At a certain point you're going to have to meet your girlfriend's social circle. You've been putting this off longer than that digital rectal exam you promised your primary care physician you'd endure four appointments ago. You'd rather be out on the lawn with a flashlight hunting for gophers in the sleet. You adore this woman on some level. There is no logic tree to detail how you might adore the other people that she adores. When her college roommate is yammering on about her rescue dog and the how vegan organic mayonnaise tastes just like Kraft's chemically optimized masterwork, stay focused. Pretend like you want to be there. As with the rectal exam, breathe through your nose and relax. You're taking the stand in an important jury trial. Do not look bored; it makes you look guilty.

For these types of meetings, secure a neutral battleground. Upscale restaurants are strategically solid, but pose a financial problem. Her second cousin just returned from a Peace Corps stint and hasn't had a decent meal for two years. A double order of surf and turf later and she's adamant you all split the bill. At risk of looking cheap you need to throw down your credit card without a hint of hesitation. You're having sex with her cousin. She knows you're good for the tab. Get used to this arrangement.

The key is not to have to endure the stories. Your girlfriend thinks by never telling you about her previous boyfriends, she's sparing your feelings. What you wouldn't give for some sordid sex tales by way of her ex-lovers in lieu of having to sit through an evening with a friend of hers from work friend giggling about that time that guy did that thing. Pretend you're far more spontaneous than you actually are and suggest an activity to distract from a conversation that will eat away at your soul. Bowling works. So does, an arcade. Possibly a guided burro tour. Maybe you all meet for drinks at the local sports bar. You couldn't have foreseen the noise at the place for Game 6 of the World Series. Smile often and don't get caught watching the game.

Make sure you meet her friends at an evening venue. Brunch is absolutely out of the question. Brunch is a weekend meal designed solely for you to have to endure your own family, not others. Friendly brunches result in bottomless mimosas and belligerently screamed anticlimactic stories about a bitch whose name you can't make out that is either "Susan" or "Shoshanna". You'll anxiously look around the room but there is nowhere to go, not even in your mind. You're bolted to that table and there's nobody to blame but yourself.

Instead, pick something as late as night as possible. Mention how badly you want to meet her dear friend, but you can't get there until 10. Show up at 10:30 and apologize. At 11:15 make your first suggestion that it's late and you have work in the morning. Women respect a man who will turn down

THE BEGINNER'S GUIDE TO MANHOOD

another round to be ready for work in the morning. That's not you, but tonight it is.

If you're in line to meet her parents, tuck in your shirt, plaster on a fake smile, and ride it out. They're not going to like you. You're penetrating their daughter twice a day, once on the ride over to meet them. They were once you. They know this. They'll size you up within five seconds because most of their work has been done in advance with background checks.

If you're employed and have no criminal record or serious credit problems, they already find you acceptable. Parents don't want their daughter to be happy; they want her to be cared for by somebody other than themselves. They might try to shake you with an in-depth grilling about your career track or that uncle you have who committed a rather serious felony, but remain steady. Use vague adjectives like "strong" and "promising" to lull them into a stupor. They're probably thirty years your senior. Use that to your advantage. Have you mentioned that you have work in the morning? Time for the doggy bags.

Occasionally your girlfriend will have protective male friends who will try and size you up. They've known her since high school and they think of her as a sister. That only means they've never been able to have sex with her for all of their big brotherly treatment. They represent far less threat than you might imagine. Confess to them you're a compulsive gambler with a penchant for Thai massages, it doesn't matter. Nobody cares what the guy in the football jersey and stupid hat thinks. If they mention anything to your girlfriend, be sure to let her know how jealous they are that you landed the best woman on the planet. Problem solved. She will now let you try that thing you've been mentioning since your fifth date.

On the ride home from any of these events to meet her friends or family, she'll turn to you and ask for your honest opinion on the people you just met. Do not give her your honest opinion. This is very much akin to when she asks you, "How do I look in this dress?" It's only a trap if you're extremely daft. Grin the perfect width and declare that her friends all seemed fun and she's very lucky to have grown up in that family. Next time you'll be busy reprogramming the garage door.

Marry Or Don't, Don't Sit on the Fence

Men used to get married young because women's liberation had yet to open up to them an array of willing sexual partners in their 20's and 30's. You got married because you liked your high school or college girlfriend, and her family had a job for you. Also, you couldn't have intercourse until you did. And intercourse seemed like a really neat idea.

The modern man knows when it's time to tie the knot. Not because of a special tickle in his tummy or because he's been planning his wedding day in his diary since third grade. A man surveys his romantic relationship and the tension is palpable. She just stabbed that head of lettuce to death. No man wants to get married anymore than he wants to eat carrots, get his prostate checked by a physician talking about sports to ease the tension, or grow out of watching professional wrestling. Yet all of these things are good for you. So is marriage, in general, and statistically speaking. There's no shame in strategic surrender. Every great military leader has a sensible retreat on his curricula vitae. Swallow your medicine and stash some money in your crawl space. Not every decision in your life need be for the sole benefit of your cock or wallet.

Make your proposal simple. Avoid hiding the ring in a champagne glass or dolphin's blowhole. It's a contractual offering. You're an adult. You wouldn't enter a business meeting with a proposal that could only be uncovered after eating through a layer of marzipan. Pretend it's spontaneous. If you blurt out "will you marry me" over a beef and cheddar sandwich at Arby's, she'll remember it forever. There's no better form of relationship credit than that garnered for being thrifty. Avoid getting down on one knee. This isn't the victory formation. If she agrees to marry you she will soon have near complete control of your life in a practical and legal sense. Enter this arrangement standing. You won't be so fortunate upon exit.

Marriage proposals should be a private event. Guys who hijack a Jumbotron or an entire restaurant's attention or engage their friends to execute a complicated dance number to propose to their lady are not romantic, they're showboats. Their karma comes back to them many times over in the form of every future romantic gesture never attaining the same production value. If you don't believe she's going to mention that once or a thousand times, then you might be dumb enough to rent the Jumbotron.

She's already agreed to be your girlfriend for some extended period of time. There's a good chance she's either enthused about you as a husband, or in the very least, settled. A legendary proposal isn't needed to get you over the finish line. Just ask.

Some people recommend spending three months' salary on an engagement ring. Those people are typically sales representatives in the diamond industry. Do some reading. They exploit child labor in Africa. Prepare a short PowerPoint presentation for your fiancée and Photoshop some tears onto the poor orphan boys if need be. Those people aren't getting three months' pay or even the remaining balance in your PayPal account.

Search for something quaint and vintage on eBay. Deliver it with a story about how your grandfather had only a tin washer with which to ask your grandmother to marry him. They lasted sixty wonderful years. Dab, don't wipe, your eye. You just saved yourself fifteen hundred dollars.

Men Are Too Smart for Office Romances

Not once in the history of mankind has having sex with a woman from work turned out for the best. In the minute and random chance you end up married with many babies and a happy home, your exception has caused karma irreparable damage. Following ninety-nine percent of office flings, you will not end up happily ever after; you will end up averting eye contact at the copy machine thrice a day until one of you quits. If you happen to be her superior she'll get you fired once you inevitably lose interest and she reports your indiscretions. If you are her peer your boss will fire you in a jealous fit because he had a crush on her. If she is your superior she'll fire you simply because she can and you'll never work in that town again. Harassment lawsuits will ensue. You'll make everyone you mutually know and work with feel utterly awkward. Half of them will drop you as even a work friend. This could have all been avoided.

The basis of office romance is not passion, it's laziness. It's the same reason guys have sex with the neighbor or the girl next door in the dorm or their female roommate or the nanny or the cleaning lady. There are a literally over one billion eligible single women in the world. Stay away from the twenty or so you see every single day. A man doesn't choose which mountain to climb based on proximity to his bus stop. Leave your residence and place of work, get out there, and meet women more than one degree of connection removed from you.

Put in some effort. The odds your soul mate works in the cubicle next to yours are exceedingly low. As are the odds she is head-over-heels for a fellow grunt. When you meet somebody totally new, you can spin your viability as a potential mate as positively as possible. The people at work have seen you drunk at parties and borne witness to your occasional bathroom low points. There's no room for spinning.

For any sage advice given to a man, there is the devil on the other shoulder pushing him toward copulation. Inevitably your loins will vote against your own survival interest and you'll end up having a toss in the sack with the cute girl from accounts payable. Understand the risk you're taking and be prepared to cut ties with your job, your apartment, or your marriage, and walk away. In the very least, review your lease agreements before agreeing to go out for comforting margaritas after her boyfriend dumps her. Keep any workplace relationship casual. Tell her more than once that we're just having a little fun. Maybe you're not ready to commit yet because your wife recently died in a freak scuba accident on your honeymoon. Act unstable and unfit to be in a relationship. Talk about your bankruptcy and your drug problem. Any lie to keep her at bay. With any luck you'll be able to break it off without serious repercussions and have a comfortable hug at what used to be called the office Christmas party. She will have to be the one who ends it or else you're the one in the precarious position.

Keep office hookups on the down low. Public displays of affection could be your demise. Tell her you're not ashamed and you don't care if people know, you just want it to be our little secret. This phrase will turn her on and she'll resort to sexting you during work hours while peeking at you from over her three-quarters bullpen wall. Eventually you'll be found out. This is inevitable. Hopefully by then you've developed an exit strategy and can escape unscathed. Feel free to believe the entire office and the head of Human Resources aren't speaking about you behind your back. They are. Imagine the sound of a ticking time bomb in your head as a means of visualizing the ACME dynamite stick ignited in your work pants.

In the history of man there are two unequivocal pieces of advice that shine above all else. Pack extra dry socks and don't crap where you eat. Even dogs instinctively follow the latter. The measure of a man will never be how prolific he is in his sexual exploits, so much as how well played.

Porn Sex Is For Porn Stars

Many men learned the freaky-deaky arts from watching pornography. While porn is awesome and healthy to view and as American an institution as apple pie and packing heat, it's a fantastical film genre, not exactly realistic. Many of us discovered this the hard way when we first began having sex with someone other than ourselves.

How many of us grabbed a girl's boobs hard and squeezed thinking that they would writhe in ecstasy only to be yelled at for bruising their teat? Or were met with icy silences when we asked about backdoor entry, or having gained access to the sacred place, then asked for an oral chaser? How many of us have thrown our back out trying to achieve all those Twister game positions? The porn star is not a normal human. The gods have blessed them with the ability to screw in ways mere mortals can only imagine. A number of awkward positions they assume aren't comfortable even for seasoned sex athletes. They need to allow a clear shot for the camera of their business doing "the business".

You shouldn't think pretending to be a cop or a horny stepson is an acceptable form of foreplay. Yet there are three lessons from adult entertainment that a man can incorporate into his sex life in a practical positive manner:

Make it original. Men are going to get off by just rolling on top of their girl and grinding away like a pug on a sofa cushion. But that's not hot for you or her. Find some ways to make it exciting. Role-play, romance her, or bring in power tools. Light bondage, or Barry White records. Boredom is the death of sex.

Stay in shape. Most porn stars are in physical shape, which makes sense since their job is to be naked. You don't need to have rock hard abs like a gay porn star, but if you did, your woman would be begging you for sex, not the other way around. Try and be more fit or at least suck in your stomach for the two minutes she bears witness before you jump on her. "But Ron Jeremy is fat and messy!" you might say. True, but he also has a 12-inch dong. Do you?

Foreplay. As men we can all agree that any intimate contact not involving penetration is not only boring, it's counterintuitive to our genetic instinct. It may seem nonexistent in porn but you are sadly mistaken. Even in modern porn there's time for the leading-up-to-banging mutual pleasing. You cut off the foreplay and you will find yourself getting less sex. It's that simple. You'd climb Kilimanjaro to get laid, so why not spend five minutes pretending you're the captain of the Love Boat to get to the same goal? When a man is faced with an unpleasant chore that needs to be done, he gets it done, with a smile.

Remember, you're not dating a porn star. Though should you ever find yourself with the privileged opportunity to bang a porn star, you better pull out all the stops. The boring Wednesday night three-minute hump with your socks on that flew with your ex is not enough. Take whatever pharmaceuticals you need and make sure to stretch. You are representing the lot of us. Don't let us down.

A Man Never Fools Around With His Buddy's Woman

Men are not monogamous by nature. It is a man's natural inclination to sleep with as many female sexual partners as possible. This isn't about pleasing your junk. This is about survival of the species from prodigal fornication.

When the modern man finally decides to butt heads with nature and settle in with just one woman, this is not something to be taken lightly by himself or his social circle. For the man who has boldly, rightly or wrongly, chosen the path of monogamy, it would be an especially heinous crime for one of his buddies to ever become intimate with his chosen mate. A friend's girl is simply off limits. It's the least you can do for the poor bastard.

Some more ambitious men may argue that no women are off limits. If a woman has a special man in her life, it's her obligation to be faithful, not the marauding pirate's. While it is technically true you have no obligation to commitments made in any other man's relationship, if you sleep with his girlfriend, you are absolutely mortal enemies. A man would never be friendly with the man who slept with his girlfriend, though he may challenge him to a duel and leave him to die choking on his own blood. That gurgling sound in your soon to be lifeless trachea is the dulcet tones of what you should've respected in the first place.

Rick Springfield wrote about pining for his best friend's girlfriend. If your buddy has landed himself a woman who ignites your primordial reproductive fires, tough luck. It happens. Try spending less time around him. Don't tell him why. There's no way to explain it that won't cause complications and destroy your friendship.

Luckily we live in a country where people break up all the time. Your buddy's girl may not be your buddy's girl forever. How long you have to wait to take a crack depends on how close of friends you are and how long they were together. Here's a simple system for calculating how long you have to wait to have sex with your friend's ex:

If you attended or would have been invited to the wedding and sat on her side, then Half Time (if they dated two years, you have to wait one full year);

If you attended or would have been invited to the wedding and sat on his side, then Even Time

If you attend or would have been invited to his bachelor party, then Double Time

If you were or would have been the best man at their wedding, then Never. Some male bonds may never be broken.

These rules may seem strict, but they represent an important note of etiquette in the world of men and male friendships. How interested you are in being a man's friend dictates how long you wait. If you want to be good friends, hate his ex. If you want to be blood enemies, nail her the night you help her move her stuff out of his place. Life is all about choices and consequences. Don't double down on Man Rules violations without accepting the consequences. Above all else, a man lies in the bed he's made without complaint.

Men Do Not Sext or Share Dick Pics

When a man is organizing a sexual liaison he should be discreet and careful to not incriminate himself. A simple invitation to meet is a tried and true method. There is no need to detail your anatomical specifics or outline the various sex acts you hope to be participating in. Aim to impress the woman in person, not with Dear Penthouse letters relayed via text message. Imagination is a powerful tool. You're ruining it with your insistence on bullet points.

A man does not leave a paper trail of his dalliances. Rest assured she will be reading your messages aloud to her girlfriends as a form of one-upmanship, or post-breakup, to mock your ridiculous sexual lingo. What sounds enticing when you're rearing to go is without fail somewhere between corny and creepy the following morning. The difference between a naughty boy and a pervert is truly the circumstance of the man and woman in question

Under no circumstances does a man send a woman a photo of his penis. Consider first the practical ramifications. That photo will end up on the Internet. Your parents have the Internet. They should never have to see your penis again after you start wearing big boy pants. This makes for awkward Thanksgiving. For years we've been urging teenaged girls to be far more reticent about sharing intimate photos of themselves in order to be liked or popular. You're not a teenaged girl, you're a grown man, and you shouldn't require the same peer pressure speeches from the PTA.

MAN RULES

Photos of nude women arouse men. It doesn't typically work the other way around. The site of your hairy veiny member does not put her in the mood. That's why she keeps inviting you into the darkened bedroom while you keep on insisting upon the 3x500 Watt spotlights you've set up in the living room. You've either watched far too much porn or you simply are denying common sense for a very personal cheap thrill. Your naked Johnson leads her to compare its appearance to various zoo animals and consider lesbianism. She may even encourage you to continue sending photos. This is not because she's busy pleasuring herself, it's because she's in need of additional laughs. Or, if you're a Congressman, she's setting you up. She will forward at least one to a friend with a funny caption and it's a matter of time before your junk goes viral.

Above all else, sexually explicit text and certainly dick pics are gross behavior. Not that sex is gross, but being overtly sexual when not in the direct presence of your mate is gross. A man is never gross. Nor is he the willing and stupid participant of a future blackmail scheme that was so very simple to avoid.

Women are attracted to mystery, not photographs involving tape measures. Do your dirty talk in person. Check the room first for wiretaps. You're certainly not filming any of this because a man never captures images of his bare ass. That rule is sacrosanct. Sex tapes aren't healthy for anyone. You've got 10,000 to choose from online made by professionals. Let everybody do the work they trained for.

EXTRACURRICULARS

Your Bachelor Party Isn't Your Big Night

Before a man ties the knot he must get together with a bunch of guys and participate in activities that might ensure the marriage never happens. The point of the bachelor party is twofold: You need to wake up once more sans pants in a $69 a night hotel room to fully appreciate your soon to be wife; and you need to confirm you're getting too old for booze and whores. She could be bringing you a Gatorade on ice right now; instead Chad's testicles are uncomfortably close to your face. The bachelor party also represents a litmus test for your intended bride. If she's got a problem with you jetting off to Vegas while your cellphone goes dark, maybe she's not the one. If a lap dance or a couple of illegitimate twins can end this relationship, perhaps it wasn't meant to be. Love is a delicate rose. You likely won't do these crude things again once you're married, but you don't want to concede you're right to do so.

The overriding rule of bachelor parties is that upon their conclusion there is no evidence of what took place. Leave no paper trail outside of the line of crumpled ones leading to your suite. Keep your phone in your pocket unless you're ordering an Uber or an ambulance. Never underestimate how dumb your dumbest friend is. If your buddy carelessly tries to take a photo of the stripper dressed as your ex girlfriend smack the phone out of his hand like he's a toddler with a throwing star. Nobody takes pictures. Pictures end up on Instagram and women scroll through phones when you're on the riding lawnmower fantasizing you're in the Grand Prix.

Be vigilant, and wary. Ask "who goes there?" when approached. The wives and girlfriends of everybody in your Bacchanalian expedition will be texting them with leading questions like, "So, I heard Greg was playing with some random girl's boobs." She's fishing. She knows nothing. You wouldn't give a fake PayPal account deactivation email your social and birthdate, don't bite on this. Text her back and tell her you're just hanging by the pool and maybe going to catch a movie. It will drive her insane and she'll break her own phone.

For that certain feeling of special, your bachelor party should take place out of town. There's nothing more depressing than watching a guy sign his life over after his last stand at the local Dave & Busters. Not everybody has money, but you can find places within and outside the borders with super cheap travel deals. If possible, fly to a third world nation where your phone doesn't get service and you have zero chance of being spotted by her childhood friend who she invited to the wedding

Even with the hall pass, implied or direct, don't push things too far at your bachelor party. Ideally you want to rage hard enough to justify suspicion, but nothing that would bring charges. You're marrying your wife because you've had enough of untoward women making off with your best concert tees, so don't jinx the deal. There's nothing wrong with cocktails and witnessing broken women shed their clothes for a group of men while each of you pretends this is entirely natural. If you've got barnyard animals or blood involved in any way, you've gone several steps too far.

You're likely to have that one guy in the party who insists on doing something super crazy. Adopt a strategy of harm reduction: barricade him in the bathroom wait him out until dawn. Even if you're intrigued by the sinful plan he laid out using room minibar liquors, the one night your fiancé will question you about forever is not the night to give life to your darkest secret. Save it for a random Tuesday night two years into your marriage. Being obvious is merely an acknowledgement that you lack foresight. A man never charges blindly into the breach. Hit the Jacuzzi and try to relax. Save room for the wedding, you'll be drinking hard.

Grown Men Don't Have Birthday Parties

Once a man reaches a certain age, he ceases having his friends serenade him with Happy Birthday over cake and ice cream. In most industrialized countries that age is six. If you're still delighting in birthday clowns by third grade, you're probably a fetishist and should consider pre-emptive counseling. A man knows turning a year older isn't a significant accomplishment. It's like watching Big Bang Theory re-runs. Even if you make a concerted effort to avoid it, it's still going to happen. A man saves his celebrating for winning a parlay at the horse track, his serenading for sea chanteys, and eats cake whenever he damn well feels like it. Childhood behind us, men can stop the sentimental charade of being lauded, feted, or honored for surviving a calendar year. Women are sentimental by nature, and remember something insensitive somebody said at their birthday twenty-three years earlier. It's important that one of the genders holds forcefully on to the past, but we are men and men move on.

A man does not invite people he knows from work or the bowling league to come to a hole-in-the-wall nightclub and bring him token gifts. That's the second-rate thinking of a second rate-king without real accomplishment. Men don't dream in color and they don't need to feel special. When a man opens a box with a bow on it he prepares for concussive explosion or live snakes. Stop raising his blood pressure.

Birthday Dinners are a disaster in the making. They have drama baked in. Men don't like drama and they certainly don't like baking. Your waiter is high and can't possibly maintain thirty orders right. At least half of your acquaintances are petty thieves who'll skip out on their share of the bill. The guy who orders the sushi served on the bellies of Brazilian models is adamant you split the tab evenly. Your decent buddy with two kids and a mortgage drowning in debt just got stuck paying ninety-seven bucks for two PBR's and three chicken wings. Now his children have no shoes until spring. Some friend you are.

If a man feels like attending a ball game or going to Vegas because it's Asian Ass Week at Binion's, he just does it. It has nothing to do with the calendar or the biological clock. Everybody has a birthday. All seven billion people on the planet have birthdays every single year. You're not a princess, you're a man, and you don't have time for shenanigans because you need to get to Denny's by the stroke of midnight to cash in that free Grand Slam.

All that said, there's nothing wrong with a simple acknowledgement of birth anniversary. It is acceptable to announce that you'll be having drinks at a bar around a certain time. Never a precise time. You're not a watchmaker. Come by if you want, or don't. You're not going to have sex at the end of the evening, so your ambivalence is completely founded. Save your trinkets and baubles. The only acceptable gift to give or receive from another man on a birthday is drinks. Just enough to forget you've not accomplished half of what you'd expected by this age, but not enough to get blubbery about never getting that matchbox racer as a little shaver. There is nothing more useless to a man drinking away his pain than cake. Peanuts are more than fine. Cashews when you're dead.

Men Don't Attend High School Reunions

In high school you were friends with guys for an entirely circumstantial set of reasons. You were teammates, or they scored the best weed, or they had a working car, or their single mom traveled a lot for work and didn't freak out over taco stains on the carpet. You also liked pretty much every girl with developed breasts. A decade later, you're still friends with a small number of the ones you really liked. A high school reunion is merely a large assembly of the ones you didn't.

Once you graduate high school, the thought of returning should not cross your mind. That includes dating the girls and certainly not sending out mass emails to your former classmates to organize an official rendezvous. High school class reunion committees will begin targeting you with enthusiastically phrased reminders about anniversary events within a few years of graduation.

MAN RULES

Consider the zeal with which a salesman sells his product inversely proportional to how much you really need that product. The guy slinging crack in the alley won't so much as list a single benefit of his product. The high school reunion emails will contain effusive hyperbole that would shame a Mormon missionary. If it were so obviously awesome, wouldn't I know that?

The only people interested in going to a stuffy, awkward adult prom are men who peaked in high school and the socially awkward teens who were universally ignored and used this as fuel to open several child sweat shops. The quarterback who's stocking merchandise at his dad's hardware store won't attend. The chess club President with designs on world domination that owns a basement effigy of Chelsea from first period will definitely attend.

Most graduates fall somewhere in the middle. They had a few friends in high school, are gainfully employed, and have no interest in talking to people they politely friend then un-friend on Facebook whilst hovering over pigs in a blanket in an airport Marriott. If you still live in the same town, you see these people in the grocery store and pretend you're on the phone. If you moved away and are making a special trip to attend instead of going to Cabo you should be detained at the airport because you're insane. This is not a knock on memorializing past events in your life. This is a knock on doing so in the most superficial and cliché way possible. This is human scrapbooking. Men don't scrapbook.

That being said, if you had a raging dandruff problem in high school, wore your younger brother's hand-me-downs, got duct-taped to the flagpole during homecoming and are now the CEO of Apple, show up with a Victoria's Secret model in something inappropriate. Have a brief exchange with the dude in the stained tie who fucked with your locker. It won't make the bad memories go away, but at least it'll give people at this tiresome event something to talk about. Though that guy in the stained tie will probably kick your ass in the parking lot. High school lasts forever.

You're Too Old For Halloween

Dressing up in costumes is the strict purview of children and woman excited to show off the results of their latest gym routine. Have you recently worked off the fat rolls between your breasts and armpits? If the answer is no then there's no reason to be excited about that revealing superhero costume. Nevertheless, there will be certain times in a man's life when refusing to wear a costume will make him more stubborn jerk than principled hero. It's a fine line. If people in your life vocally declare you jerk, you've probably crossed over the line.

Whether it's Halloween, St. Patrick's Day, or a bravely resisted but ultimately succumbed-to jaunt on a medieval themed cruise, costumes along with gift wrapping are a rarefied moment in life where a man is best served doing the bare minimum.

While it's tempting to show up to the Halloween party in your stained sweatpants it's not a viable option. You are declaring yourself anti-costume, which you are, but the idea of costumes must be condoned so that women continue dressing in lingerie outfits with feline or sponge-nurse themes. To thine own self be true is wonderful advice if you never plan on bedding a woman in your life. Being subversive doesn't work either. Every disaffected male has had the notion of wearing a snow hat and announcing they're a ski lift operator. It's more annoying than clever. The guy who's been meticulously Amazon Wishlisting the historically preserved components to his Attila the Hun outfit is going to soak up even more adulation while you're alone on the patio sharing seven-layer dip with the raccoons. His and Her costumes should be avoided at all costs as this sets the precedent that you're going to start bringing matching centerpieces to the cookout. It's also more binding than an engagement ring.

The same costume rule goes for minor occasions such as those Ugly Sweater parties your least funny friend throws every Christmas and the annual Jimmy Buffet concert you attend instead of a mandatory seminar at your work conference. Wear a green shirt on Saint Paddy's day and pick up a novelty sweater. There is no appropriate gear for a Jimmy Buffett concert except a length of garden hose for your tail-pipe. For the same reason this book will not cover appropriate behavior in a Bulgarian men's sauna. You've untethered from the mother ship. You're on your own.

A man knows his costume doesn't make him the life of the party. A clever costume will never make up for a lack of charm and humor and social graces, at least not until the party attendees are substantially intoxicated. A costume should only be enough to keep a man from punching the third person who asks what he's supposed to be, and increase the likelihood he'll be able retire to his shabby couch to indulge himself in that brunette who dressed like Pocahontas assuming porn was thriving in the 16ᵗʰ century.

If a young lady should ask a man to participate in a kinky game of escaped prisoner and the Warden's wife, all bets are off. Man Rules are meant to be broken. A man must assess how passionate the woman is in this matter and realize what goes around comes around. You can be an NFL QB for the night if it means making your ultimate fantasy of frequent, no frills fellatio come to life. Nobody likes a man who takes himself too seriously. You can fake it three nights a year.

Fantasy Football Is Everything Not Manly About Football

If a man has a hankering for football he plays a pickup game with his buddies. He doesn't fantasize about sports from his recliner. A man's fantasies involve hauling in giant marlins or committing unspeakable acts upon a former Disney teen TV star are kept private to the grave. If you're fantasizing about men in football gear, keep it beyond the grave

Men watch football on Sunday. They drink more than they initially intended and yell at the television, and then wake up Monday morning and go to work. Unless they work for the NFL or an NFL franchise, they don't spend their every waking minute poring over football stats. A man cares about the number on his bank statement and maintains a rough estimate of the number of children he has. He's not concerned with working out mathematical equations in the name of pretend time. He can tell a good quarterback solely by jawline. Numbers are the devil's folly. Also among the things he had more time for when he wasn't responsible for his own rent.

MAN RULES

A man will end up joining a fantasy football league at some point in his life in the name of camaraderie and because his wife doesn't know he's gambling with the car note. When naming his fantasy team, a man doesn't use cute puns such as Brady Gaga or Party Like A Gronk Star. He's already decided he doesn't have the time for any of this and goes with something practical like Team 7.

While engaged in fantasy football play a man devotes no more than a few minutes a week to his managerial duties. Ninety percent of that time should be dedicated to aggressively insulting the other guys in the league. None of them can throw a spiral. No topic is off limits, including mothers and that time Jeff ordered a daiquiri and thought nobody would notice. A man proposes trades exceptionally sparingly. Trades among men are reserved for necessity goods to make it through the winter, and in the old days, women. Your ancestors traded pelts for jerky. Tobacco for molasses. You just traded a backup running back for a place kicker. Your forefathers would've committed themselves to never engaging in intercourse if they could have seen you pounding the table with that fantasy deal.

Men never speak of their fantasy team in social situations because they realize that as conversational topic it's well below gas prices and canker sores. You might as well discuss the omnibus bill working its way through the Senate or your new living room set. Your wife spent three months picking out that furniture and deep down even she doesn't care. Women have their own burden. Nobody likes the guy glued to the TV during a thirty-point blowout because he needs an extra six rushing yards. No matter how comfortable you feel in a public setting, don't blurt out your fantasy team results.

When a man wins his fantasy league he doesn't gloat. Nor does he sulk when losing. Have you ever seen a male lion sulking? Keep that thought close to you in moments of defeat. A man understands fantasy football is largely a completely random game of chance and no more than one step removed from Dungeons & Dragons. He takes his league winnings and spends most of it on drinks for his friends.

Everybody should be encouraged to make a pledge to not to do this again next year and instead drink rum and attend a bullfight in a Spanish-speaking nation. You will have grandsons one day who will want real stories. Fantasy football will not measure up in any way to that time you become inebriated and ran into the bullring and spent a week in a foreign prison.

Men Gamble In Moderation

The thrill of winning will never equal the pain of losing. It's nature's way of keeping us from resting on our laurels. When you visit a casino the odds are you'll lose. Guys who tell you how much they won never count how much they lost. Professionals don't play with their own money and you're not a professional, you're reading a Keno pamphlet. Gambling is an occasional source of crude entertainment that inevitably loses you money in the long term. No different than visiting a strip club. Luck is not a skill and chance victories are not laudable. Pulling three cherries is not an accomplishment. Honor this reality before you walk through the brass doors.

You're not the only one who suffers when you gamble away your future kid's college fund because you let pride get the best of you at Caesar's. Think of your buddy from back home who's been looking forward to this trip since last leap year. You moping around for the next seventy-two hours in a previously worn bathrobe is ruining the vibe. You're scrounging money for room service pancakes while they're out enjoying free highballs. You might not be invited next time. And it's your wedding.

Don't gamble with money you can't afford to lose. Take your yearly gross income and divide it by a hundred. If you're Jay Z, that's a million bucks. Your gambling honeypot is sizably smaller. That's the upper limit of what you should be spending on any given gambling trip of which you should have no more than four in any given calendar year. Spread it around. There's no need to dive into a twelve-hour poker game upon getting your room key. Start slow; grab a subsidized French Dip and a beer, chill. You'll do better at any activity when you pick your spots versus engaging in compulsive behavior

If you find yourself reciting the Rosary before each hand of twenty-one, it's time to walk away. The more you're counting on winning, the less chance it will happen. That's not objectively true, but it will feel that way and you'll suffer all the same. Casinos aren't built on miracles; they're built on math and the pensions of people with oxygen tanks. The fleeting rush of adrenaline can be an addiction every bit as dangerous as cocaine or those little packaged pies.

If you find yourself hitting the downtown casino on your way home from work or texting in bets on women's basketball you need to stop. If you can't stop you need to get help. Gambling will ruin your life and the lives of others around you. It's a vastly underreported scourge that takes a man by the collar and won't let go. You can revisit the hobby when you're thinking clearly and

THE BEGINNER'S GUIDE TO MANHOOD

not counting on luck to pay your rent. A man knows that you earn what you need in life, you don't win it by spinning a wheel and counting on a random outcome. If you happen to win a few bucks, upgrade to the seafood buffet and tip the waitress with the mouths to feed. That investment pays out better than craps.

A Man Keeps Himself Busy Outside of Work

In every tired slogan there is a nugget of truth. "Idle hands are the devil's workshop" is a bit dramatic, but if you've ever known men with too much time on their hands, you've seen the workshop in all its demonic glory. Free time doesn't mean watching the paint dry. It means freedom to choose what you do with your time outside of work. A man employs his freedom to keep himself in a superior state.

A man should schedule a certain recurring endeavor to keep him balanced and out of trouble at least once a week. A challenge to complete in order to calm his nerves and keep him grounded outside of his hired labor. Regardless of whether you're driving a long-haul truck or working on the Space Program, you need something you can grapple with, leave it all on the mat, and return to your routine.

This extracurricular activity should be something communal, like a regular poker game or a basketball league. Happy Hour doesn't count, and neither does fantasy sports. Humans must sometimes come together for a greater purpose than just getting lit or playing pretend. Hunkering down in your basement for hours on end fashioning antique arrowheads defeats the purpose of socialization and normative behavior. Links between Ham Radio operation and pederasty is well researched and documented.

When left to their own devices men tend to resort mostly to gambling, womanizing, and the obsessive-compulsive tracking down of rare comic books. Also drinking. Drop in some time on your local novelist. They're all collecting yarn and slurring by noon.

Isolation is not meditation. You might find enlightenment alone into the woods for the winter to test your survival skills. Counting the holes in the drop ceiling tile and vaporizing marijuana is not the same thing. You need to leave the house. Nobody ever takes a deep breath and puts the controller down when they conquer a video game. They keep playing video games. You need something that can be completed session by session. Masturbation doesn't count. There's no championship. Black Belts in martial arts represent a mastery of mind, body, and spirit. It has very little to do with being able to kick everyone else's ass, although that's probably a factor.

If you're not a team player, consider singular athletic endeavors like surfing, lifting weights, mountain biking. Physical exertion is good for the spirit. For those looking to exploit loopholes there are many activities that also involve a degree of booze or womanizing such as bowling and dart leagues, rugby, and, God forbid, tribute bands. Have a place where you can find your Zen after being informed the valet who parked your car just totaled it. This is the time where you turn your phone off for an hour or two and concentrate on the task at hand. Dedicate yourself to this project at least once a week. Put it in your calendar. Mark it sacred.

Men Shun Romantic Comedies

Romantic comedies are movies decidedly for women. Period. It is not that men shouldn't like these movies; they should have no opinion on them whatsoever because they should never have ever seen one in the first place. Romantic comedies are emotional, lighthearted, loving, and a number of other qualities men have no use for, or understanding of. There is no movie genre less manly than romantic comedies. There are only two days a year it is acceptable for a man to watch a romantic comedy: Valentine's Day and his wife's birthday. Even then, it has to have been her idea, and he has to ruin the occasion by relentlessly ridiculing how bad the movie was until she feels stupid for even liking it.

More congenial men do not think watching romantic comedies is worthy of concern. Other, more plotting men will put forth, "If all I have to do is sit through a bad movie for two hours and it will make my wife happy and get me laid, what is the harm?" Hate not their naiveté even as it rots our planet from its core. Romantic comedies are more than just bad movies. Adam Sandler movies are just bad movies. Kate Hudson movies are penis kryptonite.

Every romantic comedy follows the same formula: An otherwise successful and superficially beautiful woman doesn't have a man in her life. She feels like something is missing and is discontented with her life until she meets the man of her dreams sometime in the first thirty minutes. This is where romantic comedies attempt to trick men into thinking that these movies are not so bad. In the beginning, the male lead is typically a real man. He drinks beer, watches sports, curses, farts, hangs out with his buddies and overall is pretty cool dude.

The heroine spends the next hour of the movie trying to change him into someone completely different. A paltry, weaker version of a man that she and her shallow and bitchy best friends think is a suitable mate. Eventually, she discovers that despite her best efforts the man still acts like a man and she leaves him. The man tries to find joy once more in strip clubs and pick up basketball games but finds them empty, perhaps the most pernicious falsehood of the genre. He decides that he can't be a man anymore and change on his own. He makes some substantial romantic gesture based on the delicate arts he learned in her presence and awaits her approval. Once she is assured he has sold out his gender and thirty-seven forefathers, she welcomes him back into her tender bosom.

Romantic comedies teach women that a man is only a decent mate once he willingly suspends the better part of his manhood for companionship. This is the obvious though never spoken aloud message of nearly every romantic comedy ever made. These films brainwash women into believing that any man can be molded into a new character very much like Play-Doh. When men agree to watch these movies, they are virtually rubber-stamping this view on gender and relationships: That men should only be afforded sex once they've lost all respect for their own penis. It's more sad than ironic. Subscribe to this view and you've just bought yourself a lifetime of colorful sweaters.

The Sports Bar Isn't Your Safe Space

It's easy to imagine that a sports bar is the ideal Margaritaville to live out your days. There are multiple televisions tuned to sports, rivers of beer, waitresses in tight t-shirts, and everybody pretends that nachos count as a vegetable. There will come a moment during a visit to your favorite dive where you and your friends will raise your schooners and swear you're never leaving this oasis. You will. It closes. Also, the pay sucks.

A man may prefer to take in a sports match in the comfort of his own home where the beverages aren't marked up for retail sale and the broadcast sound isn't muffled by a massive herd of angry townies. On the plus side, at the local sports bar your discarded wings are scurried away by a pie faced coed instead of remaining on your counter until the next round of the playoffs. Your buddy's wife won't give you a hard time if you make a mess in the bar, as if she's never vomited on a duvet during a ceremonial keg stand.

You need to carefully measure the pros and cons of visiting a tavern on game day. You can see the picture better on your home flat screen than from a Cinco de Mayo decorated booth with sombrero clad frat boys stumbling across your eye line. If you've wagered your firstborn's college fund, have a nagging case of Asperger's, or are writing a feature article about the defensive scheme for tomorrow's paper, stay home. People at a bar will watch the big game on one TV and midget golf on another, all while trolling for anonymous sex on their phones. Women don't typically pay much attention to the game, even the ones with NFC North team names tattooed on their foreheads. People at a bar are going to talk to you. Aside from getting drunk in the dark in the middle of the day, that's the whole point of a bar.

If you're a diehard fan and this is a seminal moment in your life, it's best to avoid a place stuffed with amateurs. There are certain bars that will cater only to your team. It's because they're desperate for drunks. Rest assured you could find a Miami Dolphins bar in the Pacific Northwest. These places tend to attract obsessive-compulsive types who are still angry at their high school coach, and a reasonable number of women. Identifying as a sports fan shouldn't be more important than your baseline level of self-respect. The game comes before all-else but a few times a year. It can't be every Sunday, that's a seventh of your life dedicated to sweaty men who don't know your name and don't care.

Learn how to pace yourself when drinking during a game. You should probably stick to beer. This isn't a late night bar hop and there's a good chance you'll be sitting there for six hours. Drunk people are more obnoxious in the daylight because there isn't an amorphous cloud of them around to blend into. You're not trying for full-on drunkenness but rather Aunt Linda after one cup of eggnog.

Sartorially speaking, don't treat the bar like dress-up day on The Price is Right. If there's one thing women dislike more than a crew of men dressed exactly the same it's a junior marketing manager stumbling around during daylight hours with tears streaming down his face paint. A jersey is fine if it bears the scars of history. No sweatpants. You're not warming up on the sidelines for a fourth quarter substitution. You're a thousand miles away with hot sauce smeared on your face.

Imagine yourself as the quintessential European who appreciates sport as an expression of culture. Of course that's not true. You want to beat your chest and fart openly while chugging beer cheese sauce. You need to stay home with your underemployed friends if that's the case. Faking it is a large part of becoming a man.

A Man Travels Adventurously

A man is inclined to explore the world around him whether that be inspecting his alley for raccoons or visiting Tanzania to witness the breathtaking natural beauty of Lake Victoria. Men are genetically programmed to become frustrated and disenchanted with their current surroundings. This is a large part of why you can't stand your roommates and they can't stand you. Huddles were intended to be informative and instructional, and last three seconds, not six years of taking turns with the remote and accidentally sharing socks. Whether driven by primal urges for adventure or insanely clickable travel deals, a man will at some point be circumnavigating the globe in the manner of his migratory ancestors. The corner bodegas were very poorly stocked ten thousand years ago.

As you travel abroad you will come to realize that America has a reputation in the world akin to the cigarette-smoking bad boy in high school. Everyone admired his independent streak, but talked shit about his upbringing after his routine suspensions. As an American traveling overseas you're a target for passive-aggressive interactions from people who can't put their finger on precisely why they don't like you but are dead certain they don't. Most of the negativity you attract is from people who are jealous of your lifestyle or were taught the Holocaust was a hoax in kindergarten. The United States is the richest nation in the world. It's easy to forget that when you're living paycheck-to-paycheck and eating Oscar Meyer cellophane-wrapped snacks.

The brutish reputation Americans enjoy is somewhat deserved. Many of your fellow countrymen walk around with their chest out demanding that a bistro in France produce a gluten-free chilidog for their obese child. It's the byproduct of coming from a plentiful land where an unruly mob doesn't form to burn you alive if you insist upon creature comforts. Try to recall that truly spoiled girl you loathed growing up. Use her as a baseline against which to measure your tone and attitude while asking the staff why the toilet flushes funny in your hotel room.

Don't assume foreigners speak the King's English. You were a barely passing student in English during the bulk of your educational year and it's your native tongue. You don't speak a second language, not even a comprehensible phrase in Spanish after spending the past three years working with Mexican-Americans and watching soccer on TV Azteca. When you're visiting a foreign country the onus is on you to communicate intelligibly. Grab something from your hotel with the address printed on it to help out your cab drivers. Have an app ready on your phone that translates key words. Those old travel language books that taught you how to say, "Where is the train station?" or "Can you direct me to the discotheque?" seem silly and anachronistic, but now you can't find the train station or a decent place to dance so the joke's on you. All of these methods are superior to raising your voice in English and assuming that screaming is tantamount to a universal translator.

Don't be snobbish about local customs. If you want American norms while in China, go to P.F. Chang's. When abroad, try eating pickled fish for breakfast; it's not going to kill you. You just chugged a bowl of cheese sauce and your heart is still palpitating. There is more than one right way to do something. Your way and this wonderful new way. You possess the testicular fortitude to try weird things with an open mind.

Xenophobia is a natural and even helpful part of an overall security posture. Remind yourself that you volunteered for this trip. You weren't tricked into a van with the allure of free video games and whisked off to Ulan Bator for a roasted rodent smorgasbord. Under no circumstances should you complain that the bed is too hard or that the local chef doesn't know how to prepare native dishes properly. This will insure you will be scorned or ignored for the remainder of your stay and possibly pummeled with nunchucks in the alley. The point of traveling is to experience new things. You could have stayed home and watched reruns of Married with Children. Though don't. A man doesn't recognize the word staycation. Nor does Webster's.

When traveling, attempt to blend in as best as possible. Avoid safari hats and strapping a Civil War-era silver nitrate flash camera to your back. Tourists are invariably highly targeted saps and a natural mark for opportunistic thieves and gypsy children who will bear a more politically correct identifier by this book's second edition. Lose the Bermuda shorts and make an effort to moderately blend in. If you're sticking a plate in your lip you've gone too far.

That Rosetta Stone on tape tutorial didn't work as well as you think. Trust me.

Traveling to distant places provides you the chance to reinvent yourself, even if but for a week or two. Get drunk and grossly plagiarize comedians you saw on TV. You can claim the entire breadth of Jim Gaffigan's material as your own and nobody in Indonesia would be the wiser. Choose your new backstory wisely. Think playwright or bridge engineer over hedge fund manager or drone strike coordinator. You want to come back alive. Unless you've already shared all the good photos on Facebook, in which case, everyone will note your demise as unfortunate, though not tragic.

Vacation Like You Need a Break

When a single man goes on vacation his main objective is to eat some steak, drink an unnecessary amount of beer and watch TV to the point he's no longer hell bent on quitting his job. He wants to wear the same pair of shorts the entire week and sleep sixteen hours a night in the starfish position. He's not a museum-goer in his real life and he's not about to start now. However, the lone survivor liturgy becomes moot when the vacation involves a significant other.

Packing is a woman's favorite pastime narrowly edging out worrying and planning. She'll have a footlocker the size of a zeppelin queued up a month before the trip. She'll provision for herself at least one cooking appliance and a Ziploc baggy full of vital documents. A man can't even name a vital document. He throws socks and underwear into a convenient sized bag and forgets most everything else. His ancestors owned a single loincloth for travelling that served as wardrobe for both day and night. Be sure to bring your wallet, your phone and a charger. Everything else is easily replaceable. You can gloat when the airline informs your travel companion that her bag was lost in the war. If she's nice, maybe you'll lend her your '92 Devils jersey to cocktail hour. Assume you'll be toting the equivalent of luggage for the entire Duggar family across at least four miles of foreign soil. Pack your own wares accordingly.

A man does not participate in hotel or resort activities. Basketball is technically an activity, but nobody calls it that. Hula dancing lessons are an activity. You have to walk the line between personal pride and a potential argument. Pick something you want to do and preface it with the word "romantic". For example, maybe we should try this romantic shark-feeding thing? Keep the planning to a minimum. If you find yourself struggling to make an appointment, you've forgotten the point of vacationing.

When men vacation together the objectives change from relaxation and intercourse to competition and survival. The guy who says he's going to "take it easy" the first night inevitably ends up face down in a pile of his own vomit outside a strip club the police could swear they shut down years ago. At least one of your friends is mulling a divorce and has made a suicide pact and wants to take you all down with him. When the subject of an off-the-grid after hours party comes up you'll know someone's had too much. The old adage of liquor before beer holds true. Similarly, cocaine and ill-conceived overseas car wash investments go hand in hand

Living dangerously is for the other guy. Live smart and say nice things at his funeral so you can have sex with his bereaved widow. Dying young is for rock stars and athletes who have wonderful stories to tell in Heaven. The highlights of your life have yet to happen. Don't end yourself in a Cancun two star you found on Priceline.

Video Games Are Satan's Man Test

The classic stereotype of gamers paints them as sexually frustrated unwashed nerds who live in their parents' basement. As with most stereotypes, it's largely true. The more video games a man plays in his adult life the further down he tends to reside on the socioeconomic Donkey Kong ladder. Don't perpetuate the stereotype. Level up. A man should not have six hours available a day to dedicate to shooting digitally rendered men or winning fake Super Bowls. Don't force potential mates or employers to measure you against men who do that for real.

Gaming can be addictive. Benders involving Tijuana sister hookers may be more exotic, but you can still lose your livelihood from the comfort of your couch. When you plug in that box understand you're taking a major risk. Fixation is not something easily predicted. A week may pass and you'll have nothing to show for it but a shirt full of Frosted Flakes shards and a notice on your door saying they shut off the gas. Video gaming is a narcotic. Some people experiment with drugs at a high school or college party and laugh about it twenty years later. Others are still at that same party at thirty-five.

Even if you are able to self-regulate your gaming play time, remember that video games are pure masturbation. If you find it relaxing, that's wonderful. If you find it relaxing to the tune of several hours a day, you're masturbating too much. You stopped smoking pot and doing donuts in the parking lot. This is part of the evolution. Women see that console and an alarm goes off. Does this guy eat at Chuck E Cheese and collect Pogs? You could cite the competitive world of eSports, even though you have zero connection to the profitable component. Having a wicked backyard Wiffle Ball curve doesn't merit you Kershaw money. Therefore, you should not quit your day job to join a Wiffle league in Tucson where you dominate the competition by day and sleep in your car by night. Climbing Everest is a thing. High score is not.

Video games are not without their obvious charms. Having a Street Fighter tournament can liven up a party and is a great way to make one of your more tightly-wound friends start crying. Find a glitch in the game and exploit it. Refuse to play another game when he demands to even the score. Any pursuit that causes other men to become emotionally overwrought separates the wheat from the chaff. A man instinctively maintains a list of which members of his social circle he wants in his army. Not the guy who throws the game controller. He will get you all killed on Day One of the Great War.

Outside of locked-down trailers at various U.S. military air bases, nobody has ever changed the world with a joystick in their hand. No woman ever has ever screwed a guy because he dominated at Halo. If you're not impressing women and you're not earning money and you've become chubby and pale and you have tendonitis, it's time for some soul searching. The outside world can be challenging and even harsh, but at least when you kill people, they stay dead. Also, the smell of cat poo is less intense.

Maturing as a man doesn't mean surrendering all connections to youthful indulgence. It merely means moderation and prioritization. A man puts in more than he takes out. Mass consumption is never admirable, especially when it comes at the cost of your most precious commodity, time. How many epic tree houses could you have constructed in the time it took you to complete the Grand Theft Auto 5 Beach Bum DLC Expansion Pack? Don't let "Game Over" be your epitaph.

STANDARD MALE BEHAVIOR

Men Are Assertive, Not Assholes

Some men are natural leaders and others are genetically imprinted to be followers. That's how we all eventually proceeded out of the wilderness and why there are tons of bar fights. Whether aggressive or passive, men believe themselves to be unequivocally right about everything including how to spell Albuquerque when arguing with that city's mayor. Confidence provides a survival benefit. It ensures that a man won't be lost in a haze of self-doubt when surrounded by danger. Here's what needs to be done. Are you sure? Not in the least. But it's better than doing nothing. The wafflers get eaten. Eventually the tribe gets more self-assured.

All interactions between men involve an implicit power struggle. It could be something as trivial as your buddy passing you the asparagus or as critical as your dental technician using his own avant-garde technique despite several ultimatums from his superiors. Men are designed to constantly test one another. We no longer butt heads literally. We troll with wider nets. It's constant and often more brutal in its subtlety.

A man needs to feel that every minor transaction is a negotiation he either vetoes or generously allows to proceed. Like a benevolent dictator or your dad. If a guy with enough testosterone gets a job in a Baskin-Robbins he'll sooner resort to pretending he doesn't speak English before readily scooping another man's ice cream. Conversely, if asked for directions by another man, he'll lay out a series of navigational processes and celestial directional reckoning not seen since Magellan.

When you criticize another man, there's going to be pushback. Remain calm, never flustered, smile. Smiling is disarming and much more productive than resorting to arm wrestling. Salesmen grin incessantly by design. Otherwise some guy would pile-drive them. Use the sandwich method. Open with a compliment, slip in your actual point, and slap another pleasantry on top. For example:

"David you're doing a great job tarring my roof. It appears you're using chocolate cake frosting instead of traditional tar. That's not up to code. Otherwise your technique is superior to that of a young Wayne Gretzky. Here's the tar."

Men are ego-based creatures. If you didn't know this from your own experience, tune in to any women's talk show where they are discussing men. They have it figured out. Stroke a man's ego and he'll be delivering your newspaper with a bow on it instead of shooting it through your living room window with a T-shirt cannon. Men love to have their asses kissed. It's a sign of submission. Engage as needed. There's a fine line between an obvious brown-noser and a successful salesman. Aim for the latter and you'll be living in the big house.

The Golden Rule has never been trumped. Treat others how you would like to be treated and your life will be much easier. Everyone has someone they have to answer to and someone who tells them what to do. Guys who are rude to waiters take longer to get their food. That's how life should be.

Men Are Never Cheap

There is a difference between being cheap and being thrifty. A responsible man doesn't spend more than he has and tries not to get into too much debt. A cheap man buys two-ply toilet paper so he can pull apart the plies and have two rolls worth of butt wipes. Cheap men buy their kids carcinogenic Chinese knock-off toys for Christmas and never ever take their lady out for any meal that doesn't involve a coupon or an extra value menu. A thrifty man is worthy of respect; a cheap man only derision.

Cheap men don't tip well. Even if you've never worked in the service industry, you know that servers depend on tips to supplement their substandard salaries. It's an odd labor market, but so it has been for centuries. A man tips twenty percent as a rule, or more if you were more than satisfied. It's the very rare case where you should leave less than fifteen percent. Did the waitress shit in your salad? No. Leave her a decent tip. She is absolutely not performing this job because she loves the work.

Nothing in the world is a bigger turn-off for the ladies than a cheapskate. Crying is a close second. Human evolution has ingrained in women the overriding mission to seek out the best provider. Being cheap shows that you are more of a self-interested individual than a man who provides for others. If you're stiffing the bellhop at the hotel, how does she think you're going to take care of her mom in her golden years?

For a man, money is a function of pay, which is a function of time and effort. How a man spends his money is a strong indicator of the priorities in his life. A man takes care of himself; he does not take care of himself to the exclusion of others. Overspending is male heresy. Under spending is unattractive. Find the middle ground where you're generous, but not a fool. Give her neither beluga nor borscht. Man always searches for the sensible middle on domestic issues that he inherently poorly understands.

Men Are Cool, Not Hip

There's no shortcut to cool. A man should convince people he's interesting through his thrilling personal stories, amazing accomplishments, and his impromptu ability to play the tenor saxophone even though he's never mentioned it in the five years you've known him. You cannot become cool just by smoking hand rolled cigarettes or hanging out in used record stores. Like knighthood, you can't identify as cool, others must bestow the title unto you.

The term "hipster" is entirely misleading and often misconstrued to be synonymous with cool. There was a time when hip and cool were indistinguishable. There was also a time men wore polyester shirts without irony. Times change, as do social mores. Hipsters consider themselves cool in a self-referential pyramid scheme in which they've all committed to lie to each other. Being stuck up about music doesn't make you cool. Playing bass guitar instantly does. Buying used books doesn't make you engaging, just insufferable. Try writing a book about seventeen daring hours you spent pinned down in the mountains of tribal Afghanistan. Now that's cool.

Buying a Jet Ski or massive flat screen television can make you cool for a few hours. Material consumption carries some allure in a materialistic society, but that hype is a mile wide and an inch deep. Your friend just bought a Porsche. There goes your flat screen allure. There are no vintage clothes you can buy, no crusty old dead person's camera you found in a thrift shop that will make you cool. If you want to honor the greatness of the past, call your parents or grandparents and explain to them you're getting a real job.

Many men gravitate toward superficial trends in hopes of covering up the obvious, that they're not very impressive and they were the kid who smelled in high school. Every few years there's a new trend to jump on that offers a cheap ticket to social acceptance. Today that trend might be man buns and tribal tattoos. A man must constantly ask himself, is this who I am or is this who I'm trying to be to fit in? If it's the latter, it can never be cool. Fonzi never polled his friends on what he should wear.

A man should embody his own personal style, not copy someone else's. Most men who have a signature style didn't put a lot of thought into it. People first noticed the man's excellence in some capacity and only then started tallying up his cosmetic characteristics in order to mimic. If I wear Michael Jordan's shoes, I will be Like Mike. It's an infantile belief in causality that is perfectly acceptable before you reach high school age. A grown man should understand that to be a better basketball player, consider thousands of hours of practice. Wear any shoes you like.

A good deal of stylistic cool was born of necessity or circumstance. Nineteen-fifties hoodlums wore blue jeans because they were issued them in work farms, just like ill-fitting baggy pants were issued to future hip-hop stars in prison. Seventies rock stars employed scarves and opera-length gloves to hide track marks and dark sunglasses to mask pinned pupils. Similarly, if you are a lineman for the county and wear work boots and a tool belt, you are cool. Not so much if you are a business intelligence analyst for a search advertising start-up.

You don't see a lot of materially successfully men wearing scarves and eyeliner. It's because they don't need to. Make enough money and your Target store white briefs will become your registered trademark. Cool guys don't advertise that they're cool, because it's obvious. Just like men comfortable with their sexuality don't brag about the size of their penis. Confidence is amazingly quiet and essentially cool.

Conversely, being a nihilist slob who throws beer bottles at his walls doesn't make you cool by exclusion. Decrying every convention of society as false and artificial displays an inability to think profoundly. Life is nuance. So is cool. Zero tolerance policies are idiotic by definition. Show a level of discernment about the world around you. A man appreciates nice things; he simply doesn't let them define him. Find some clothes you like and stock your closet with them. Get a vintage dartboard or even a record player if that's your thing. Before you know it you'll have a style that is all your own. If it involves leather chaps you did it wrong, go back to Start and try again.

Men Try Hard, Not Too Hard

A man naturally desires to separate himself from the rest of the herd. Masculinity is a uniform baseline from which to climb your own mountain. Everybody loves a true character. By the same measure, everybody abhors a poser, a phony, or any man whose primary trait is trying far too hard to be noticed.

As a rule of thumb, avoid behaviors that are overtly trendy. You'll become a walking punch line. Stay away from anything favored by guys who forever need a couch to crash on. Practice good hygiene. Personality goes a long way. Truck Nuts do not. Consider this list of nine public behaviors to drop immediately. It's hardly a complete review, but start here and you should find your social circles, romantic relationships, and financial prospects dramatically enhanced.

Cigarettes. Smoking is a dying habit. Most women find it repulsive and nonsmoking men no longer find you cool. Your apartment smells like a French soccer club. How did you get here? The nicotine sensation is now far outweighed by the negative social stigma. Cigarettes became popular because they were considered rebellious. Now we've all seen the cancer lung photos. If you think sucking on an electronic version of this very same habit is a manly alternative, you have bigger issues than a book can address. Men don't suck. Repeat that until you're blue in the face.

Look at Me Hair Hairstyles. Outside of small fraction of the population who maintain their hair according to their Lord's will, skip the trendy hair arrangements. Man buns, ponytails, and most notably, dreadlocks. Dreads signify but one thing: you have dirty hair. Well, two things, your hair is dirty and you want everyone to know. Men become unclean and odorous in the construction of grand buildings and watercrafts. Not in the pursuit of using their hair as their primary form of accomplishment. If you want to change the system, run for office. Good luck with dreadlocks.

Sunglasses Indoors. Unless you're afflicted with an ophthalmological condition or you are Stevie Wonder, wearing dark glasses indoors causes you to resemble a guy who just killed a hooker and knows his mug shot is on the news. It's a hostile act that says you base your fashion sense off of rebels in old movies. Most of those characters were in high school; you're nearing your fifteenth reunion. There's no way to pull this off without looking like you made the conscious decision to feign badass. That never works.

Tank Tops. If you're building sandcastles with your nephew or hitting a dive bar in the summer, tank tops are cool. Once the sun goes down you look like a guy who beats up on the paperboy or the paperboy's mother. People notice your armpit hair and correctly assume you're showing off your muscles. This can come off as desperate. The same goes for any undersized shirt. We can tell you're flexing. Until we figure out why men have nipples, it's best to not make them a highlight of your ensemble.

Weird Tattoos. Any permanent ink above the collar or below the wrists signifies you're part of a dark underbelly. This is acceptable if you're fronting a successful death-metal band yet poses a problem when applying to the investment bank. Everybody regrets these five minutes after they're now a forever part of your body. Make a pact with your friends that whoever is the least drunk keep everybody else away from the tattoo parlor. If you must tattoo to honor mom somewhere about your ankle or foot or privates, do that. When you've been inducted into the Yakuza or landed in a Russian Gulag, you may revisit the placement.

Novelty Clothing. Funny guys don't wear funny shirts or hats (or have funny nicknames for that matter). A "Hooters Inspector" ball cap doesn't make you the life of the party. It makes you feel awkward when you're standing in the corner convinced people are staring at you. They are and they are not thinking good thoughts. That "who farted" t-shirt that served your reputation well at seventeen doesn't hold at twenty-seven. Everything changes when you need a decent job and a decent woman. So do the rules on novelty clothing, bumper stickers, rear view mirror ornaments, and ornate water bongs. Tone it down, Randy.

Owning a Pit Bull. Having a dog capable of killing small children is acceptable if you have an estate frequently under attacker from the Visigoths. It's not necessary for your modest weed stash or $299 TV from Best Buy. Your dog is largely intended to be fun loving and a good way to meet women. As to the former, almost all reasonably sized canines serve the purpose of being amazing companions in need of relatively little maintenance. As to the latter, think furry and adorable. Your dog doesn't want to be euthanized for infanticide; he wants to be a conduit to you getting laid. That's why he's man's best friend.

MAN RULES

Anything for the Sake of Irony. Irony works when your audience is well familiar with your frame of reference; more specifically, all your existing friends and co-workers. And they've already seen that joke. The ugly sweater is hilarious, it's just those ten guys with funny mustaches in the corner already thought of it. That tired adage about being yourself is something every man ought to repeat to himself until it's even more tired. If you're not inherently cool, a Tony Orlando tuxedo is never going to help.

Toilet Humor. Don't be the guy utilizing bathroom humor as his go-to material in social circles. No matter the immediacy of reaction from those around you, you are certainly confusing abhorrence with adulation. It's like you took the world's oldest joke and shoved it up your ass. Being crude in context has its merits. Clearing out a room with a fart and a giggle speaks for itself. In fourth grade this made you king. In your 20's it means you're not getting any. A man is always seeking to raise his game and never settle on cheats. You could learn a few new legitimately chuckle worthy jokes every now and then.

As with all lists in this book, this is hardly comprehensive. Merely the obvious deal killers. If a couple people seem to have a problem with your behavior, you might just be onto something. If everybody seems to have a problem, you're being an asshole. Honest self-evaluation need not be constant, but once a month it's a good time to take five minutes for a check-up.

Sometimes A Man Has To Shut Up and Step Up

Gender equality is a sign of human progress. But equality remains a cultural phenomenon, not an evolutionary outcome. In practice, there are certain jobs men can do better than women, in general. And vice-versa. This natural distinction upsets some people who would wish it otherwise. Let them be upset. A man knows that enlightenment and realism are not mutually exclusive and he's willing to suffer for this knowledge.

A man takes on the dirty work in his relationship with a woman. This doesn't exactly smack of equality but if you plan on maintaining any type of relationship with a woman you're going to need to bear the brunt of the physically arduous tasks, save for bearing offspring. That's no small concession.

A man plunges the toilets, cleans out the garbage disposal, scrapes ice off the windshield, and assembles a thirty-piece bedroom set from a single diagram poorly printed in both Swedish and Tagalog. You have two options: do it, or let it sit on the floor until you're forced to carry it to the dumpster, which is again your duty. Moderate swearing is fine. Allowing your woman to reach into drains to extract old chicken wing bones is not.

Anything involving heavy lifting is squarely on you. Loading the car, moving furniture, carrying the luggage, pumping the keg, mowing the lawn, and freeing a hiker who is pinned under a boulder. A man would never look to a woman and wonder if she's doing her fair share of the grunt work. You are the grunt. She is the woman who will nurse your babies and one-day change your diapers and see that you leave this planet with some dignity.

Driving falls under this banner as well. While driving modern vehicles is more light touch than physical application, men remain superior drivers to women on the whole. No matter how accomplished a horseback rider the princess, the knight rarely rode bitch seat on his own steed. Is male-female tradition outdated and patriarchal? Have your wife answer that question the first time the car gets a flat in the rain.

The man should handle matters of conflict. Women seek pragmatic solutions and dialogue and should be encouraged to seek peaceful resolution. However, when your neighbor's visiting buddy has jacked your parking spot for the third night in a row, you are the one to go over there and tell him if he does it again, there's going to be a problem. If the restaurant host tells you there's a wait for a table and then seats the people behind you, you need to confront him. The same goes with disciplining the children or the dog.

For better or worse, men are more programmed for violence and therefore more physically intimidating and threatening. Certainly you know some very scary women, but it likely took a while for you to make that assessment. Your first impression may have noted their sweetness and pleasant demeanor. Versus the guy chesting you up, snarling, and reaching for his machete.

There's a fine line between chivalry and sexism. Men inherently will never understand that fine line so make your best effort and try to ignore the barbs of simplistic binary judgment. Women don't need you to open the door for them. Do it anyway. You'll sleep better at night knowing you did at least one thing today in the manner of your grandfather.

A Man Does Not Tolerate Unemployment

Men were built for near constant toil. Don't believe what you see on gaudy reality television shows, almost everybody is busting their hump almost every day. For all the complaints about incessant hard work, men with regular full-time jobs register much higher on most every quality of life issue. The man who wonders what he's doing this Wednesday and next Tuesday for the next three years is in for some depression. Seasonal catamaran tour operators being the exception. Really anybody who gets to wear sunglasses attached to Croakies around their neck during the performance of their job can take off six months without much concern for their mental health.

No matter the fault, there's a time in many a man's life when he finds himself out of work. It can be devastating to tell your loved ones you were canned, let alone turn down a steak dinner with the guys for fear of overdrawing your account. As with any setback, the key is to limit the lamenting. Men don't lament problems, they find solutions. Getting laid off is a temporary setback. It's not the time get that Mohawk you've always wanted and start a punk band through Craigslist as those financially dependent upon you become increasingly concerned.

Banks used to remind everybody to save for a rainy day. Now they encourage you to spend more than you have and pay on credit. A man should really focus on the former. Good credit is like good hygiene. Conversely, bad credit is like an STD. Women with options can read your FICO merely from your countenance. When you are employed, you need to save money. That doesn't mean living miserly and pinching every last penny. It means considering whether that latest flat screen is necessary when you have no cash on hand for next month's rent. You always hear about the guy who loses his gig and almost immediately starts sleeping on the street. Sometimes you do get snake bit, almost all of the time you completely ignore common sense and reasonable planning. A man should never be caught ill prepared.

Tenacity is how you won that bloody knuckles competition in middle school, and it's how you're going to find your next job. Employment hunting is inevitably a humiliating process. As humiliating as courting a woman, but you don't get the woman should you succeed. It's easy to surrender after numerous passed over resumes and initial interviews. Before you know it you're sleeping until noon and wearing your bathrobe to he convenience store, drinking Miller Light in your apartment with the lights turned off and playing video games, as you wonder why you haven't been laid in a year. You need to pound the pavement. Call upon friends and friends of friends. Network. Social network. When all else fails, just hanging out is a positive step. Are you looking for a job fixing cars? There's a bar those guys frequent. Shower first, and go find it. Get out of the house. You may be a couple rounds of tequila shots away from the place you'll work for the next twenty-two years.

If you qualify for Unemployment take it but be weary. Cashing checks that barely get you by is not a job. You'll burn through it and be right back where you started. There's nothing worse than borrowing money from friends or

THE BEGINNER'S GUIDE TO MANHOOD

family. Many of them will tell you to get it together and they're right. Next thing you know you're not on speaking terms with your mother because she suggested you manage the neighbor kid's lemonade stand while you get back on your feet.

Setting realistic expectations is important. Don't be the guy who hasn't worked a day in the last twelve years because he can only imagine himself carving statues outside stadiums and there haven't been any openings. That doesn't stripping or cleaning toilets at the Taco Bell, though a real man would do either to feed his family. If you're holding out and not getting any bites, you need to make some adjustments. If it's been a few months, find a full time job you can tolerate to pay the bills and continue pursuing something else in your free time. It's always easier to find work when you're currently employed. For the same reason attached guys find girls easier. Or the girls find them.

There is no shame in working any job. There is shame in the reverse. If you find yourself watching The Price is Right, you're on the short end of that equation.

Men Don't Drive Electric Cars

Much of the social evolution of the past generation has focused on assaulting the traditional male culture. The term traditional male culture itself now connotes boorishness, feudality, and a propensity for bouts of violence and stupidity. For the vast history of humanity, traditional masculinity meant hard work, honor, and self-respect. The unisexual onslaught from preschool on up has affected what men say, what they wear, and how they act. The emasculation of maleness peaked when it started affecting what men drive.

Automobiles are amongst the manliest machines known to man. It is an insult to men everywhere to drive an electric car. Cars represent pure raw sexual power in the form of the combustion engine, with its driving pistons and potent torque. Electric cars represent the dull hum of a couple D-batteries made in China. One man surrendering his manhood affects all men. Imagine an offensive line where just one lineman decides rough contact is abhorrent and allows the pass rusher through. The other teammates have their dignity, but we now have a dead quarterback.

The sex/power relationship to automobiles does not mean a man should buy the biggest diesel truck available and put 22-inch wheels on it. Unless you are a WWE star or South American drug lord, riding a monster truck in the city is an obvious sign of overcompensation. Driving a convertible doesn't make your hair grow back and driving a big truck doesn't make your penis any larger. A gas-guzzling raised truck is really no more manly than an electric car as it circles back upon itself in the masculinity universe that is definitely not a line. Find a happy middle ground at around 24-mpg highway.

Driving an electric car is a pitiful and almost entirely symbolic way for a man to help the environment. Try planting trees in war torn arid nations or culling overpopulated animal species to aid the ecosystem. Environmentally engaged men inform their ladies that a couple of kids is more than enough offspring. Children create many multiple times the eco-waste and greenhouse gasses as a Chevy commuting to and from work.

The only thing less manly than electric cars is not shutting up about how good of a person you are for owning one. That goes double for bicyclists who have turned their personal hobby into a righteous cause on behalf of the Earth. That's certainly convenient. This Man Rule isn't about bicyclists, though if they had their way, it would be.

If you own an electric car, unplug the 75-foot extension cord cluttering up your driveway and head to your local dealership and trade it in. Toyota makes plenty of highly-rated combustion engine vehicles. Traditional cars are less expensive than your electric car, so as a bonus not only will you enhance your masculinity, you'll likely get some cash back. There's nothing more manly than a win-win.

A Man Rarely Fights

A man should look at combat the way he does attending a soccer game or using a gas barbecue. Engage only when there is no alternative. Real men don't initiate fights with other men because they understand that past their teen years it's far better to be drinking beer with women in thongs than nursing a bruised face. It's not like in the movies. Even when you win, you really lose. Everyone thinks you're an unstable scumbag and you've got a broken finger. Nobody wants to hear the play-by-play when you show up to work with a cast from a senseless fight. They just want to cancel your invite to the Christmas party.

If some scrub wants to hurl a few insults at you, it will enrage him more if you ignore his taunts than if you start bumping your chest up against him and asking him to fight. You've already lost, like the bunny that takes the carrot and gets trapped in the box. Insults almost always result from jealousy. Take it as a compliment and move on. It's much easier to walk away than to stand your ground. There's no shame in avoiding arrest or an unseen cohort cracking a chair over your head. The same losers who look to spend their Saturday night grappling another man are most often approaching levels of desperation in their personal lives. Do the math. It's a lawsuit or worse.

There are certain situations when even the most levelheaded man finds himself on the verge of fisticuffs. If some slob is repeatedly harassing your date for example, you must be clear that this cannot stand. A sober guy hitting on her is not harassment. That just makes him normal, respectable even. The threat must be legitimate, a sign of blatant disrespect. Your best option is to assert your dominance and readily defuse the situation. Regardless of what a woman says, she gets extremely aroused if you defend her from actual danger. In turn, she will not put out when you engage with some idiot to validate your own masculinity.

If you are the type of man who carries a gun or refers to his house as an armory you probably understand that brandishing your weapon should be done only in a life and death scenario. If some guy breaks into your house shoot him dead and don't let it ruin your week. If you pull that thing out in traffic you should have it taken away from you and be spanked like an insolent child. One slip of your trigger finger and you could be spending life in prison, let that weigh heavy on your mind when some evil prick causes you to apply your brakes for two seconds by changing lanes in front of you. If you take cash deposits from pawnshops in the worst part of town, you can carry a sidearm. You live in the suburbs and you're six-three. You don't need a deadly weapon.

You never saw Charles Bronson picking a fight with a guy who spends his time standing on a street corner. Tough guys don't start fights, they end them. Shows of force frighten children and associate you with common street trash. If you can walk away, you should. That said, take a few classes just in case. You'll likely have one adult fistfight in your entire life. Losing it is no reason to pick another. A record of 0-1 isn't so bad, and could even get you a shot at the title in France.

A Man Clearly Distinguishes Between Friend and Girlfriend

During grade school, boys and girls are socially interchangeable. You'll find girls playing baseball and boys making daisy necklaces and firmly resolved that Taylor Swift is the best music artist ever. A boy may have friends who are girls and treat them precisely as he would his friends who are boys. Post-puberty a man evolves his understanding of the genders and treats both men and women in his life respectfully, but not similarly. The "bro-mance" cultural meme is directly derivative of a desire on the part of many to deconstruct the natural differences between the genders. It's cute and comical, but in it's own way, as emasculating as a fanny-pack.

You don't go out to dinner with your buddy. You grab something to eat. You don't buy your friend a birthday trinket in a little gift bag. You buy him a 10-oz. titanium finish hammer. A man has no desire to attend a farmer's market with his friend because he doesn't actually have a strong passion for organic summer squash. He's faking it. Are you really looking through the weekly paper for ideas on what you can do on Sunday with your pal?

Life can't be all cooking lessons and Netflix marathons with your girlfriend nor should every night consist of farting around a poker table. You need balance in life. For this reason, you'll have to draw some lines in the sand. Unless your buddy is sleeping in your bed he shouldn't be sitting next to you on a picnic blanket. The male space has nothing to do with sexuality or threats therein, it has to do with the fact that you're a hunter, the guy next to you is a hunter, and that puts you in direct competition, regardless of the fact you may be splitting season tickets. You can't be as close to a man as you can be a woman. You may save each other's lives; you may not share your secret love of pantomime.

Women like things that are seasonal and festive and relatively insufferable. Ice-skating on a winter pond and fireworks displays on the beach. It's unclear whether this is a learned behavior or instinctive, but if it involves dressing like the Fall cover of a New England fashion catalog, women find it enticing. Men just need to sit down for a minute before hurling themselves off a cliff in a parachute. They're like sprinters. Women have more of an Iditarod mentality when planning an outing – a grueling marathon involving several stops and often relatives. She doesn't care if you get along with your neighbors you see everyday, but she wants to make sure you adore her great aunt you'll spend an hour with twice a decade.

Men forever seek a simpler life. Rules make things simple. Write them in pencil, enforce them as in pen. As a guiding proposition, do things with your

THE BEGINNER'S GUIDE TO MANHOOD

friends that your woman finds unappealing and vise versa. You could take her on a motocross trip across Baja but she'd just complain the whole time. There are no clean restrooms south of San Ysidro. You wouldn't go to a pumpkin patch with your buddy. Suggest a jaunt in the corn maze, and he'll knock your teeth in. Make yourself a chart if need be. These are my male friend activities; this is how I spend time with my lady. Hide the chart. A man plans, but his playbook is confidential.

Sports can be tricky. Some women genuinely claim to like them and may even know the rules of the game save for when to talk or be quiet. Even if they do like sports, they like something else better. Find a way to disabuse them of the notion they're pleasing you by taking part. Whenever possible, sports should be a male activity. Don't be the one guy who brought his chick. If you're not sure if it's the wrong move, wait until she tells you that you're the bigger man for bringing her. That's a gut punch confirmation. Check beforehand and don't be afraid to mark a boundary. I watch football with the guys; you and I screw in the bathtub. I'm not asking to tag along to book club.

Guy stuff is simple and requires little planning and can usually be abandoned in favor of playing air hockey in the bar. Girl stuff is usually thematic and orchestrated and can be abandoned in favor of playing air hockey only after a heated argument about the stupidity of watercolors. Men fall into the trap of assuming that women bending to their likes constitute "us" time. It doesn't and she's keeping count. The tally is probably right near that chart you hid. Date nights seem like handcuffs but they're actually a key. Suck it up and fake a smile and do your best to do things with her you'd never do with a male friend.

Lines must be drawn. Universes cannot be crossed. Men and women are different. That's not a bad thing. Exalt in the fact that you can have nuance in your personal relationships. A well-rounded and balanced set of relationships makes for an effective life. You wouldn't have a tackle box with only spinner baits, would you? .

Men Are Not Cheerleaders

Sports stadiums are the pantheons of American society. The visceral thrill of stuffing yourself with bratwurst and drinking beer through a funnel in the parking lot is indescribable and cannot be experienced through the ninety-inch flat screen you installed by crane. There's also the game.

When a man attends a sporting event he may wear a ball cap or t-shirt with his team's logo. You may wear a team jersey if you used to play for the team and are charging ten bucks for autographs at a table stationed in the mezzanine. You don't wear a white lab coat when you go to the doctor's office. This isn't your profession. You're there to observe.

Don't confuse football with Halloween and don colored wigs or capes. A man is never looking for an excuse to wear anything but jeans and a hoodie and argues vehemently against anything more ornate even on his wedding day. Face and body paint is strictly off the table. You're not fighting for Scottish independence, you're trying to hold your whizz in until the next timeout. Measure the war paint according to accomplishment. A friend who

115

wants to color a letter on your bare belly is no real friend. When he asks you to take off your shirt, smile and punch him in the sternum. This is where you let the world know you don't have trouble meeting women.

Drinking at the game is not only acceptable it's a sacred passage. Everybody sips a little Mogen David on the Sabbath. You can nurse a beer so you don't have to explain why your Paleo diet strictly forbids gluten. Your buddies didn't understand it the first fifteen times you mentioned it. That said, this isn't freshman year of college. You're trying to get Southwest-flight drunk, not Prohibition-is-over drunk. A giant overpriced beer per quarter should put you right in the sweet spot. Assuming you're not driving, in which case you get one per game. Under no circumstances does a man smuggle in a plastic bottle of Captain Morgan's or similar frat house swill because he's an adult now. Also, security is pretty tight. Too much intoxicating beverages and next thing you know you're involved in a bleacher brawl because you were arguing with the entire Raider Nation that Back to the Future II is better than the original. It's not, but there's no stopping you now.

During the game it's encouraged to yell incoherent game suggestions at the world-class professionals based on your two years of junior varsity ball. You may also boo the opposing team because all their players look like the guy who hits on your girlfriend at the Honkytonk. Cursing people's mothers and performing Voodoo chicken blood-letting rituals to cripple the running back is a non-starter. Behave with a modicum of class. Imagine what would certainly get you escorted out of Wimbledon. That's level-set behavior for American sports.

When your team wins the championship it's expected that you'll overreact and swear you'll have this date carved on your tombstone. Fortunately, the line to leave the stadium will be so long you'll be sober before you reach any tattoo parlor. Don't overturn cop cars or set fire to the Baskin Robbins. The word fan comes from the word fanatic, but you want to keep a logical behavioral gap between yourself and guys in the Middle East firing off semi-automatic rounds into the sky and whooping.

If your team loses you're allowed a twenty-four-hour grieving period where it's reasonably okay to be surly. Surly does not mean crying. Men who obtain concussions and fractured limbs for a living may cry in defeat. You just lost your voice and spent forty bucks on parking. Feel dumb, not sad. After the brief mourning period you must acknowledge how silly the whole thing is and get back to your real life, minus the vision in your left eye that was lost in the third overtime.

A Man Grows from Disappointment

A man will face both triumphs and defeats during the course of his lifetime. The measure of his grace will be his ability to be humble in his victories and to find some measure of benefit in his defeats. A man does not accept failure so much as he accepts the cosmic existence of failure. As the valley between the hills, a man rides it out high on his horse. Self-pity is never an option. A man has no time for emotions that lead to tears and herbal tea consumption. Revenge is the superior cousin of self-pity and far more useful.

THE BEGINNER'S GUIDE TO MANHOOD

The more you depend on something the greater chance it won't happen. That's not a scientific fact, but rather an estimate entirely based upon perception. Perception is not inconsequential. Nine times out of ten you're going to miss out on that promotion you were certain was coming your way, or fail to hook up with that cute orphan girl you're told loves sex but hates foreplay and conversation. Life will always hand you lemons. Losers talk about the referees twenty years after the state championship defeat. A man understands that failure is nobody's fault but his own. He proceeds to improve himself as opposed to waiting for the world to change.

Men are not made of stone. Stone weathers and crumbles. Think non-biodegradable plastic. Bend but do not break. When dealing with a major disappointment, allow yourself a brief period to mourn and decompress. This can be anywhere from a red light to an entire day. You must never retreat to the bed or consider sleep an antidote to failure. It's not. Sleep is your reward for a hard day's fight, not your boo-boo blanket when you take a tumble.

A woman might take a week to process failure and take a few demonstrative pulls from the bottle in front of company. Women do everything emotionally harder which makes their lives richer and more volatile. You're not afforded that luxury. While you're feeling sorry for yourself there's a guy out there plotting to steal all the riches you don't even realize you have. Moping is exceptionally unattractive unless you're in a band and even then it's insufferable. Lick your wounds any more than an hour or so and you're masturbating.

Any sports coach worth his salt will assure his team that losing is the stepping stone to winning. It's trite, but completely true. The Wright brothers crashed numerous times before they were finally able to take flight. Now you can watch ESPN and sip on Bacardi while jetting across the world. If you got everything you wanted you'd be married to the pretty girl you sat next to in fourth grade and working as a roadie for Styx. If you hadn't been rear-ended by that drunk driver you'd have never bedded the nurse while in traction. Baseball players get paid enormous sums of money to strike out more often than they hit. You have to be in it to win it. Never quit and you will eventually find success. Commitment is the single biggest dividing line between achievement and failure. And it's entirely voluntary.

Talk to your friends. A few minutes of your buddy rambling about his insurance adjustment job or his wife's antiquing obsession and you'll realize your life isn't that bad. Have a good meal, get some exercise and make love to a woman who appreciates the same music you like. Figure out the lesson failure was trying to teach you. Then you'll be ready to sucker punch it in the throat the next time it comes sniffing around.

A Man Is Ever Hands-Free

A man should leave this world pretty much the way he came into it. That means not clinching a Hot Dog on a Stick or a Samsung Galaxy because it looks silly in the casket. Women tote things around and occasionally haul enough weight to herniate their spine. A man keeps his appendages free. His hands must be available at all times to bat down stray foul balls or vengeful orcas. Bruce Lee didn't enter Han's Island toting a satchel and a Fit Bit.

You're the hunter, not the gatherer. Consider this when eyeing a messenger bag that looks particularly practical.

Drinks are perfectly acceptable to lug around. Men have accomplished what no other species has, engineering a means to bring the water to them rather than having to go to the water. It's why you're much less likely to die in an alligator attack than a gnu. Carrying a water bottle is permissible if you're actually thirsty, in which case you won't have to carry it around very long. If it's your comfort squeeze and you've been nursing the same liter bottle since Tuesday, that's clearly just a fetish. The same rule applies to your phone. Your phone should be used to communicate, not clutched onto like a baby rattle to distract from the voices in your head. It's okay to actually talk to people at the airport bar. They're obviously weird but they can't touch you. There are too many cameras. Don't use your smartphone as a crutch. Develop your social skills. High scores in mobile games will only get you extra power-ups, useless as tits on a bull.

Men like to listen to particularly horrible music while working out. Working out is good for you, Slipknot not so much. Store your portable devices in your pocket. You have a pocket. If you don't, it's because you're wearing leggings or bicycle shorts and you need to start asking yourself more serious questions than just about your taste in music. Women wear their music players on their arms for this very wardrobe reason. If you think doing the same gives you that Ultimate Warrior glow, you're wrong. When working out at the gym you don't need to carry around a notebook, if you can't keep track of your exercises you must leave the gym at once and complete some Sudoku puzzles.

A man carries around his own children, assuming they're under age two or had their leg caught in a bear trap. Otherwise you should teach your offspring how to walk on their own two feet or risk carrying them to class for eleventh grade trigonometry.

Women often carry their pets around with them, especially if they're infertile and believe their Yorkie to be a baby. A man leaves his dog at home to guard his stash of moonshine. When the dog needs exercise he takes it on a jog or a walk wherein he can shed some weight and his dog can hump less suspecting canines. A man knows his dog doesn't belong in a restaurant, shop, or as a comforting assistant on an airplane. If you need comfort while flying, consider a Crown Royal or three. This is the person world. Dogs will be welcome in it as soon as they understand the concept of using a credit card and not defecating in the aisle.

Backpacks are acceptable for day trips or if you're scaling the Alps. Outside of that, cargo pants, and only if you have an actual need to be carrying eleven items on your person that day. Keep your hands and feet clear of clutter. You know those meet cute scenes in romantic comedies where somebody bumps into somebody else and knocks the ton of stuff they're carrying to the ground? That somebody else is always a woman, and the $2,000 laptop she dropped never worked again.

A Man Knows When To Leave Home

It's in a man's nature to venture forth, or in the very least, to leave his past as far behind him as possible. Most mammals have a way of letting their male offspring know it's time to leave the brood. A gentle nudge followed soon thereafter by a vicious attack that takes out a chunk of hind leg. But the human species has grown comparably soft in these regards. The result is finished basements turned into bedrooms and grown men ensconced in their birthplaces well into what should be their adventurous pirate years.

There's a time in every man's life when he must leave the comforts of his childhood home and stake his own claim in the world. That time is the receipt of a high school diploma. A prison GED may provide you fewer options. By the time you've reached eighteen, you've had roughly twenty thousand meals on the house. You couldn't possibly ever pay back that tab. It's time to dine and dash. The kind the proprietors will appreciate.

If you don't already live in a bustling metropolis, you're missing the obvious. Attractive women naturally flock to big cities. They are attracted to ambition and air conditioning. There are a few quality girls in small towns but by their mid twenties they're either taken, pregnant, or nursing a nasty meth habit. Visit the hottest joint in Topeka. Now try New York, Los Angeles, Miami, or Dallas. There's an objective difference, even to the Topekans. Proximity to multitudes of good-looking women shouldn't be the only reason for choosing to relocate, though it should definitely be a big reason. Men were born with a thirst for knowledge and personal growth. Both are a distant second to the thirst for inspired procreation.

Leaving the homestead is where college comes in handy. It's a perfectly acceptable and even commendable one-way ticket out of town. If you simply leave town with harsh words regarding your upbringing, your family may disown you. If you leave for college, a random aunt will send you a twenty-dollar bill and a note about how proud she is. College is the biggest scam ever perpetrated by young people on older people who collectively choose to forget the reality of their own college experience.

Attend a school at least several hours driving distance from your childhood home, or at least one major urban center away. Skype and texts should be the obvious choice of conversation with those you've left behind. Don't move off the farm and onto a larger farm. The valuable lessons to a young man aren't found in an Intro to Mandarin class, they're learned in a speakeasy from some Mafioso who knows what happened to Hoffa. Cities have very few townies. It's one of their best qualities. That's not to say that you can't do well for yourself going big fish in a small pond. Many men choose this route and enjoy a comfortable and enriching life. All rules have exceptions. But a man knows he's never the exception. He certainly never banks on it.

People who say they can't afford to go to college are almost always people trying to find an excuse not to go. Between loans and grants and the sheer number of tax-payer subsidized institutions, there's no reason why with a reasonable number of side-job hours you can't figure out a two- or four-year college plan. If it is truly out of reach, find full-time work out of town or join the military and see the world, or at least central Ohio. Joining the military is like going to college, except you learn practical skills and leave in the black instead of in debt. Also, women will have sex with you simply for wearing your work clothes.

Sticking around your hometown and hanging out with your buddies isn't going to lead to anything except DUIs and an hourly gig as a strip club DJ. Very few people who choose this route remain satisfied with the decision. There's nothing worse than listening to a grown man cry in his beer about the Colts and how his kid was unfairly arrested by the cops while home for Thanksgiving, except being that guy. Women are nesters. Men are explorers. That's not a legal distinction; it's an instinctual difference that has allowed the human race to continue despite the flu and processed sugar. Look into the crossed eyes of people whose families have lived on the same farm or island for many generations. Now, get out and spread your seed amongst non-relatives. You can watch all the hometown parades on Facebook.

A Man Doesn't Waste College

High School is a trying time in a man's life, serving the sole purpose of pissing him off and boring him enough during his early reproductive years to start plotting his escape. College is the New World, providing housing free of parents and the opportunity to bed strange women from exotic places such as Kansas. Unfortunately, education is part of the deal. Guys who blindly pick a major based on its charm or convenience end up assisting you with your copies and slinging Cosmopolitans at the airport.

In theory, college should prepare you for the work force. Weigh your interests and fantasies versus what you actually want to do with your life. If you're keen on 18th Century poetry, read it to your heart's content and inquire with your parents as to the possibility there's a trust fund for you that previously went unmentioned. Universities will always take your money and if you give them enough they will present you with a Doctorate in the Didgeridoo, at which point you'll find yourself saddled in debt and inaccurately calling out people's names at Starbucks.

These are electives, not majors. Take a class in pottery. It's truly the best way to meet women. They'll mostly be lesbians, but that's an important experience to have at college as well. If you're into your third semester of waffling on the early works of J.K. Rowling, you're clearly wasting time, money, and prospects on self-amusing curricular masturbation.

A major must have a practical application. If your path in life is undetermined, you can't go wrong with a major that actually sounds like something grownups do for a living. Finance, business, engineering, computer programming, healthcare, or criminal sciences. The latter more so if you happen to be 240 pounds of muscle and can run a 4.6 second 40-yard dash. Does American Studies sound like a job? Women's Studies will at least get you a job at any major media outlet in New York. Astronomer is a job for eleven people in the world. Music Theory sounds impressive. Now go look up Music Theoreticians jobs on Monster.com. Nobody at college will tell you these things because they all work at college. Their majors weren't important. Going to college equips you to work at college.

Many young men are lucky enough to know exactly what they want to do. Some of these professions require formal schooling, such as doctoring or lawyering or spacecraft designer. Others practically don't. If you want to be a director there's no need to study film while at Texas A&M. Move to Hollywood and get a low wage job on a film set while doubling up with a night job delivering pizza. The same goes for building furniture or really big boats. You don't need to know Medieval French History to open a restaurant. Everything you do in your twenties will be made that much easier with a four-year head start and zero dollars in college debt.

Others must assess their potential and understand they're cut out for a life of plumbing or electrical work. Honest skilled trade jobs. Contrary to popular belief, you can actually party your ass off and sleep with women who detested their parents without paying thousands of dollars for classes. Go to a vocational school, it's the difference between being a gofer and a contractor.

If you can afford it, college is worth the experience. So is a Mercedes and it won't set you back a decade of pink envelopes threatening to foreclose on your life. Go to college if your finances and career choice support it, and understand that most of your professors are otherwise unemployable. Unless you invent a billion-dollar dating app, finish what you started. Including college. The only thing worse than a guy with a degree in Anthropology is a dropout.

Men Do Not Worship Other Men

There's no shame in a man being a fan of an accomplished sports figure or entertainer. You should be confident enough in your place in life that you are not threatened by the feats of your peers. The hunter understands that there is more than enough game in the wild to feed everyone. Rooting for your fellow man and honoring his success reveals a level of self-assuredness that present itself as calm and cool. It is the quintessential male demeanor and will encourage women to encourage you to father their children.

That being said, there is a meaningful distinction between wearing a Tom Brady jersey on Sunday and mailing a handcrafted collage of him to the address on his fan club's website. Shaking hands or having a drink with someone you admire is a realistic and completely normal aspiration. Scouring the Internet in hopes of finding where he grocery shops and then sitting outside in the car with binoculars is not. It's important to reverse the roles in the scenario and ask yourself how comfortable you'd be with LeBron James peeking through your blinds when you're shaving in the morning. Not matter how much you love LeBron James, you'd still call the police.

Esteem for any man you don't personally know should diminish with age. It's quite common and even charming to put posters on your wall and imagine hanging out with your favorite athlete or movie star in your early teens. Once you turn twenty there's actually an entry for that illness in the Diagnostic and Statistical Manual of Mental Disorders. The guy you're looking up to should be older than you are. An adult should think of himself as being in the same club with other highly successful men rather than subservient to them. This is a man just like you who puts his pants on one leg at a time and occasionally urinates on the toilet in the dark. He's not a deity and has very few answers. He's just a dude who's good at playing guitar or catching a football.

While it's acceptable on game day to don the team jersey, it should be discouraged to wear another man's name on your back. You're supposedly a fan of the team, not just the quarterback with the perfect hair. You're also mirroring the behavior of young girls with crushes on him. Any time a man's public demeanor approaches teen girl norms, it's time to consider a change. The same would go for crying while listening to music or stealing makeup from department stores.

Collecting trinkets and baubles should be kept to a minimum. It's pretty cool to own Eddie Van Halen's old guitar or a pair of Mariano Rivera's cleats and they'll display well in your man cave. However once the paraphernalia starts piling up you are rapidly building what would be considered a shrine. A man prays to his monotheistic deity for the strength to care for those under his protection. He doesn't light candles for his imagined best friend to have a wonderful performance. There's a distinction between decorating and obsessively hoarding. This would be the time to ask the opinion of a woman who agrees to give you a brutally honest answer as to whether you've crossed that line.

Every man has an affinity for certain other men who live in the public eye. When you start talking about them compulsively you are essentially admitting they would be better at banging your wife. Work on making yourself more interesting instead of insisting some two-sport star from Indiana holds omnipotent qualities. Your fantasies about Cam Newton should not be similar to those of your wife's.

Respect The Man Space

Whether he's crammed into a coach seat or hiking the great Appalachian Trail, every man needs a modicum of personal space. It's crucial to respect the area directly around another man. Human males evolved to be masters of the Earth precisely because we didn't let anything sneak past our virtual walls. Every man has an invisible perimeter around him of about three feet. That's the exact reach of a prehistoric spear.

Much like a sovereign country, when a man's personal space is invaded he gets agitated, skirmishes occur and people inevitably die. Giving another man some room to breath is the first step in earning his respect. Jabbing him with your elbows is the first step in getting a black eye.

When you come across a man who is a stranger, stay as far away from him as possible without being obvious you are doing so. This will allow both of you to get to where you're going with the lowest possibility of an altercation or impromptu arm wrestling match. This may sound silly until you realize it is the habit of every single other male mammal on the planet.

If you're on a dark street, walk to the other side. If you get on a bus and he's in the front, sit in the back. When you approach a urinal and he's on one side, pee on the other. You must have a "buffer trough" between you if at all possible. If the bathroom is not busy there's no harm in ducking into a stall. If you must sit in a public park... that was a trick. Men do not sit in public parks.

Men want to compete by nature. The closer the proximity and the greater the density of population, the greater the desire to compete. Practically, there's enough room in this world for all of you. Reinforce that point through your body language and mannerisms. An exception comes in times of war or famine. Should you need each other to survive you'll find strength in numbers. But this is a subway train; it's not quite the apocalypse. Move down a seat or two.

When you're meeting another man for the first time, offer a simple firm, yet quick, handshake. The only thing a man should embrace is the concept of being like steel. When talking to a man allow two feet between your face and his. If you see him backing up, do not encroach. Carry some gum, particularly when drinking. Foul breath in another man's face is tantamount to a formal declaration of war, and in Uruguay actually is.

Should you be on a hugging basis with a good friend, make it quick. It's symbolic. You don't need to let it linger like you just returned from Saigon. This isn't an embrace. It's a hug. There's a difference and that difference is three seconds. Under no circumstances should you ever massage another man's scapula. We've all known the guy who feels the need to give you a neck rub without being prompted. His heart may be in the right place, but his hands are not. Guess who gets eaten first when the food runs out?

Your greatest chance for violating man space comes during a drunken evening. You're far more likely to both misjudge distances and also feel like every guy you're drinking with is your greatest friend ever. You just met two of them an hour ago, but you've promised them they can hold your dad's casket when he dies. Bear down and restrain yourself from acting like a woman for whom intoxication has released a groundswell of repressed emotions. It's unsightly for a man. As needed, punch one of your new best friends in the face. Better to be kicked out or arrested than crying on the shoulder of a man you barely know because he too had his Schwinn stolen in sixth grade.

When participating in athletic endeavors limit yourself to high fives. A back slap might be fine in the event of a championship win. Under no circumstances should you ever ass-slap another man. Yes, big tall beefy old school ballplayers often do this. They also have jaw cancer and are broke from three divorces. Don't board that train unless you want the full ride.

A man should never feel the need to groom another man in any manner. You may not reach up to another man's face to grab a loose hair or eyelash. Let alone to wipe a bit of food from his face. The same goes for adjusting his collar. Make him aware of the problem and then let him handle it. You wouldn't fix another guy's fly. Treat the entire man space as sacred as the fly. You're not his mother and he's forever one step from sleeping with your girl.

When in doubt, stand your ground. If a man is heated and he finds you violating his buffer zone it's grounds for a fight. Let him cool off. Don't make things complicated. You're just trying to get your burrito and get home to watch some TV. There's no halfway into another man's space. It's all or nothing. If you wish to reduce the conflict in your life, choose the latter.

A Man Does Not Befriend His Neighbors, He Manages Them

A man's home is his sanctuary. This could be a condo, an apartment, a house, or an extended-stay motel. The principle remains the same. This is the sole space on this entire planet that is your domain. You must bear this in mind when forging relationships with neighbors to your north, east, west, and south.

Neighbors are cattle and should be treated as such. You might know a guy who knows a guy who doesn't regret screwing his secretary. Fewer and farther between are those still keen on their decision to invite the Johnsons over for dinner. When your buddy gets on your nerves you simply forget he exists for a week and everything reverts back to normal. With your neighbor this is not a possibility. They're around. They're always around.

When you meet people through business or mutual friends, they've been vetted to a certain degree. Even the guy you occasionally spot bench-press for at the gym you've seen thrice a week for two years and can pick out his body aroma in a crowd, if it came to that. The guy next door, you have no idea. He could be on the lam, have bodies in his basement, or obsessively collect igneous rocks. You'll notice you're the only one in the neighborhood who ever has guys over to watch the big game. The only people you see going into the neighbor's house are Jehovah's Witnesses and the cable guy. Take that for what it's worth.

You need to nip your openness to associate with neighbors in the bud, but even a man guarding his kingdom is ever polite. A friendly hello or a nod is good form. If your neighbor seems like a problem individual avoid eye contact and do not stop walking. Casually mention you're in a hurry. You should never be close enough with your neighbor that he knows plainly that is a lie.

MAN RULES

The typical neighbor is in constant need of small favors. Mail collection, cat sitting, jumper cables, baking soda, you're essentially their one-stop replacement for small Craigslist help wanted postings. They've achieved the impossible feat of being constantly out of town and in need of newspaper collection yet constantly playing their music too loud. And not the good kind of music. That would be your music.

Neighbors know precisely when you're walking to your car or garage and you're entirely vulnerable to impromptu conversations. Try taking your garbage out at a different hour each week--they'll still be there waiting with ill-informed gossip about other people in the neighborhood. Especially the old people. Often they have ulterior motives and are being friendly with you as a means of forming an ally in an ongoing dispute about a parking space that was assigned sixteen years ago or easement rights on a pine in need of trimming. Once you're involved there's no going back.

Many of their lives revolve solely around complaining about noise. Unless there's a watering issue, then noise is a distant second. If you live in an apartment complex, neighbors certainly have an opinion or your use of the common area after hours. Do not admit guilt or apologize in any way for your behavior. Have an edge to you and make them assume you'll probably do this again. Once you allow any power over your behavior to those you're related to entirely by random geography, they will not cease complaining until you're asking permission to run the microwave. As a general rule, make it very clear that you will not engage in neighborly dramatics and neighbors will leave you alone. If someone in a position of authority follows up with you, describe your neighbor as drunk or insane and possibly domestically abusive. Nobody else wants to deal with it either.

Occasionally you'll find a neighbor who wants to be left alone as well but doesn't mind picking up that package when you're out of town or warning you that the city has instituted a sudden Tow Away zone to raise parking department revenues. Value this relationship for what it is. Do not divulge anything personal and keep everything right on the surface. Best-case scenario, you gain their trust and never learn their full name. When the rare natural or unnatural disaster occurs, a man needs to be able to check off the other men in his vicinity to form the leadership junta that will instruct the homeowners' association watering policy Nazis on how to survive.

A Man Has But One Favorite Sports Team

A man has one favorite team per sport. Period. Friends grow apart. Couples get divorced. Asian countries seem to change their names a lot. But the bond between a man and his favorite sports team will be with him for his whole life. He must choose only one team. While a man may cheat on his life mate, he should never cheat on his favorite team. Though as in a relationship, there are certain loopholes that allow a man to be interested in a team other than his favorite and this should not count as cheating.

A man is allowed to have one team in a different conference that you "root for." This is the team you want your favorite team to beat in the Super Bowl. For example, a man might declare, "My favorite team is Baltimore but I root for San Fran in the NFC." They are not your favorite team; you just want them to do well. It's like having a female friend that lives out of town. It's not cheating, but you'd be wise to measure your connection.

MAN RULES

If your favorite team ever plays the team you "root for," under no circumstances should you "root for" that team. Even if your favorite team is 0-15 and the team you "root for" needs one win to make the playoffs, you should always side with your favorite team. 1-15 is the hill you should be willing to die on that day.

You may never "root for" a team that has ever had a rivalry with your favorite team or ever beaten your team in a major game in your team's history. You wouldn't be friends with a woman that your girlfriend hates, so don't "root for" a team that your team traditionally hates.

You are also allowed one other team in either league that you "don't mind." Typically the team you "don't mind" is a scrappy underdog from a small market that you wouldn't mind seeing win. For example, a man might muse aloud, "My favorite team is Dallas, but I don't mind seeing Buffalo win." This is akin to having a plain looking female friend as a drinking buddy. You'd never pick her over your girlfriend or wife, but sometimes she's fun to have around. As with the team that you "root for", the team that you "don't mind" cannot have ever had a rivalry with your favorite team or beaten your favorite team in a major game in your team's history. And again, it goes with out saying that you always have to root for your favorite team, no matter what.

Any man who ever knowingly or actively roots against his favorite team deserves no public hearing of his idiotic rationale, but does deserve to have his male organs cleaved from his body by a blood-thirsty alpha male orangutan. You could learn a thing or too from that manly primate. He knows exactly whom he's rooting for on every given Sunday.

Men Peruse Pornography Rather Than Indulge

No man is immune from the allure of pornography. If there's a naked woman anywhere in the world, men are interested. Socialite Peter Cook was at one time married to Christie Brinkley, cheating on her with an eighteen-year-old girl, and still maintained a regular and expensive premium online porn habit. Such is the innate passion men have for watching other people engage in sex. Not simply a substitute for real human relationships as once widely reputed, porn is a stand-alone element of male life, sui generis, a basic food group. It knows no international boundaries, age divide, or ethnic or religious favoritism. All men consume it, Individuals who publicly decry pornography are almost certainly the most avid consumers.

Pornography is not harmful in the abstract. It's a cheeseburger. A cheeseburger will not destroy your life. Ten thousand cheeseburgers is a different matter. Gazing upon a naked woman once required some gusto. The mere act of obtaining pornography was something of a challenge. Digital technology has all but eliminated those obstacles and made adult content abundant, universally accessible, and for the most part, free. Porn is like candy. Great for a pick-me-up but if you start eating it first thing in the morning it's not healthy. Free and omnipresent candy would be very dangerous for a society's general well being

A man does not require a stash of porn. Collecting baseball cards past the age of twelve is infantile. Amassing pornography in any amount is disturbing. Stowing indicates the baseline value you place on pornography and that baseline is way too high. Pornography has existed since the dawn of human existence. It's a universally desired product that makes a large number of people a large amount of money, and it's never going away. You're hoarding a non-scarce product. That makes you the much-maligned crazy lady at the end of the block they'll find one day smothered to death in collapsed stacks of newspapers and magazines. Only your stack will be pornography. Guess which case the EMTs are going to publicize postmortem with embarrassing photos.

Women understand that men enjoy pornography, but don't want to think about it, much like you'd rather not acknowledge whatever goes on with her in the bathroom for forty-five minutes while your dinner reservations are being given away. Every now and then you'll find a kinky woman who dabbles in consuming adult entertainment. Let her broach the issue before you bust out your laptop's greatest hits on the third date and find yourself being pointed out by strangers on campus.

Women will investigate your Internet history for pornography. Do not take it personally. If this woman were your daughter running a check on her boyfriend, you'd begrudgingly suspend your ardent support of the right to privacy for one evening. There's no reason for you to have evidence on your computer of any extensive amounts of porn viewing. Either your viewing is not extensive, or you're intelligent enough to routinely wipe your browsing history. Google and your ISP and companies may sell your information to fully record your every wanking moment, but they don't care about you as a potential future husband. They will never confront you in tears and ask you to explain why you visited ThreeWayEnemaNurses.com and if it means you're a serial killer or can never coach your future kids in Little League.

Women will exaggerate your porn viewing with exponentially hyperbolized impact reports. Simple lesbian porn clips will suddenly become evidence in the case for having you labeled a fetish freak and queried as to if you have a clown suit hidden anywhere in your apartment. Against better judgment, should you be compelled to store any amount of porn on your computer put it in a password locked folder or at least name it something inconspicuous such as Marketing Memos. Even people in marketing wouldn't open that boring wormhole. Minimize the amount of pornography your significant other believes or knows you to access. Saying "I never" is far too obvious. Go with "every now and then when you're out of town" and don't let your digital footprint show otherwise.

Porn watching is always a private endeavor. You do not check out sex videos while you're sitting at the dining room table or there's a graduation reception happening on the patio. A man doesn't engage in creepy or compromising conduct, most especially that involving his sexuality. You should never log onto porn sites on the bus or in the library for a quick freshening up. If you saw someone else doing that you'd never want to sit on the couches. Have some respect. Just as you wouldn't use your friend's toothbrush or dirty underwear you should never use someone else's device to look at porn. You'll probably give them a virus or forget to close a window so everyone will know you're most intimate predilections. Porn is a romantic relationship between you and your wifi. Honor it and keep it special.

Men Don't Take Selfies

Heralded explorers and daring adventurers managed to leave their historical mark without a single epic selfie. You just posted for time immemorial photographs of yourself flashing the devil's horns while attending a U2 concert. Possessing the ability to capture yourself on camera is not in and of itself sufficient reason to capture yourself on camera. Try to imagine each photo you take costs you one dollar. Or that you had to wait in line at Walgreen's for forty-five minutes to pick up your developed photos. Would you still have thirty-seven pictures of you and Steve trying on funny hats in a store? Nobody did before 2005.

The digital age didn't create vanity; it merely provided a window into the pervasiveness of the deadly sin. As if everybody in the world was suddenly asked if they had ever considered being a model and they collectively blushed and thought, why not. Women are imbued with a vain quality that can easily be interpreted as a sexual confidence. Vanity in women provides a vital purpose in nature. In contrast, the desire of some men to pose in the mirror or to document their superficial appearance can only be likened to masturbating in public. Wanting to feel special is not reason enough to be caught naked in the alley next to the bodega.

A man should be interested the world around him, not simply documenting his role in it. For those grand moments of accomplishment, the written word remains a far more powerful and lasting testament than an Instagram jpg with a hash tag. There's nothing wrong with nabbing a photo of friends and family at a milestone event. Your mom used to do this so that twenty years hence she could remind you of your cousin who turned to drugs and alcohol. But your mom asked everybody to say cheese before cell phone cameras were universally present. Of the twenty people at any event you're attending, eighteen have just taken the exact same photo and posted it to Facebook. You've already been tagged and liked and people have moved on. This happened in the course of three breaths. Your photo is almost certainly redundant and unnecessary even in the few moments it might be considered decent form.

As a general rule, don't take photos of anything that you can easily find a better shot of on the Internet or in a New Jersey turnpike rest stop gas station. This is the Statue of Liberty. Call Rand McNally. Look at that, Niagara Falls. Which one are you, Lewis or Clark? Nobody cares about your vacation photos unless your wife is very attractive and in a bikini. If that's the case, ask yourself, why are you publishing sexy shots of your wife. You don't drive a Winnebago to swingers' events over three-day weekends. Yes, it's the same thing.

At the baseball game feel free to pull out your phone and snap one shot of you and your buddies hoisting your hot dogs and beers. You're one of only forty thousand people in your immediate vicinity to be doing the very same. The key phrase here is 'one shot'. You're creating a keepsake to remember good times with your friends. You're not documenting which one of you was better at making duck faces. Women will turn a candid shot into a low rent student film. That's the difference between you and them. You attend a sporting event to watch the game; a foul ball beans them while they're sifting through the dailies. Send back the gaffers and the set designers; we all agree we were here.

As a codicil to this rule, there is simply no reason to take pictures of things that you eat. Your social circle is fully aware that you have lunch every day and that some days your lunch is better than others. A meal is not a rare event. Visiting Bennigan's isn't tantamount to spotting an Ivory-Billed Woodpecker. Order your food, have a few beers, and leave the poor waitress out of your Ken Burns melancholy retrospective on the appetizer round. She has enough work to do without touching the phone you read on the toilet.

Under no circumstances should a man take selfies. A selfie is a love letter to yourself written on expensive stationery in colored ink signed "Your biggest fan" set inside a heart next to a sketch of an adorable pony. Unless you're documenting facial lacerations from a car collision for insurance purposes, capturing your own face on camera is the height of narcissism. You've completely inverted your Maslow hierarchy of needs. Marauding simians have overrun your tribe. The people who trusted you with their safety and survival lay strewn about you dead and dying. Why not show them that shot of how amazing you look with your hair parted to the right rather than the left? A man doesn't find this analogy the least bit exaggerated.

Men inherently don't understand cameras. Men do understand weaponry. Think of your cellphone camera as a gun. Remind yourself and others that the very reason you possess one is with the hope that you never have to use it.

Carefully consider all other options before deciding to shoot. Should you be left no choice, do what needs to be done and re-holster that weapon and pray that it should never come to that again. And, by all means, never point it at yourself, even in jest.

A Man Is Mostly Sober

Alcohol and recreational drugs can be a formative part of your youth. Mind-altering substances have formed rites of passage and bonding experiences among men for millennia. It's fun to get loaded and go cow-tipping or stumble out of a bar with panties on your head a few times, yet passing out in a pool of your own vomit loses its cache pretty much immediately. Everyone gets one pass for having one too many and humping the Christmas tree. At the time it seemed hilarious, and even in retrospect it merits a solid chuckle, but history is written by those who remember it. As in all things, moderation. You don't need to be the guy in your social circle who drinks the least, but don't be the guy who drinks the most. Before you know it you are the guy who people whisper about behind his back. Remember, you share much of the same genes with your incarcerated uncle. We're all walking this earth on a fine line as to our outcome.

If partying is affecting your bottom line you need to stop for a while, and if you can't stop for a while, then you need to stop entirely. Regularly showing up to work late or getting in a screaming match with your girlfriend over Hot Pocket preparation are typical warning signs. If you're in a physical altercation with another man, odds are Cutty Sark was the cut man in your corner. If you didn't break your pelvis or lose a tooth this time, you soon will.

While not every man is a law enforcement officer or a superhero, every man is expected to be a caretaker of his family and community. A man should not have to stop for a pint before he rescues a baby trapped in a burning building.

The key to managing recreational drinking is knowing your limit. Some guys can polish off a handle of bourbon and wake up excited to shovel the driveway. These men are often referred to as Irish. Others find themselves in the fetal position talking to God with delirium tremens after a night of wine coolers. There's no shame in admitting your tolerance for alcohol is rather low. The man who can handle the most liquor often can do so because he spends all day drinking and lives in a storage container. The object isn't to get as hammered as humanly possible. Spirits should be relaxing, providing the same feeling as a round of golf, not skydiving in a flame suit. When you were eighteen there was some natural inclination to want to outdrink your friends as a sign of machismo. You're not eighteen anymore and you realize that sex and a decent apartment is more nifty than crowing like a rooster. Drink to get a nice buzz and have a few laughs, not forget your first name and beg police to arrest you. A man should ask himself, am I making people around me happy or miserable? Adjust your drinking accordingly.

Men Do Not Go Topless

A man is not squeamish about removing his shirt yet he doesn't rip it to shreds when the first UV ray pierces the morning dew. Showing up to a barbecue bare-chested means you're either homeless or pursuing a career in porn. Regardless of how many bench reps you're doing with four plates, people are going to be repelled by you. The sight of a naked man is

THE BEGINNER'S GUIDE TO MANHOOD

inherently jarring. That's how Ghandi was able to shake the resolve of the Colonial British government. They surrendered India just to not have to look at his nipples anymore.

Removing your shirt should only be a logical step to entering some body of water. There's no reason for a man to remove his shirt for any reason other than swimming. If exposing your body had anything to do with improving your non-swimming sports performance, you'd see Stephen Curry and Usain Bolt competing topless. T-shirts provide sun cover, soak up body sweat, and serve as great icebreakers at summer parties. You went to Cabo? I've been to Cabo. Awesome. Let's be friends for forty years.

Men who jog or workout topless are proud of their bodies. Men should desire strong bodies, not pretty bodies. It's sixty-four degrees out so you can stop pretending you're trekking across the blazing hot Sudan, where, by the way, all the men wear shirts. Men who love to be topless either had parents who gave them too much unconditional love, or none at all. The science is still out, though the answer is definitely not smack dab in the middle.

Under no circumstances should you remove your shirt in the ballpark. Even if you feel confident you look like a male stripper, this is a public stadium filled with men, women and children. Not the Palomino at two a.m.. People came to the game to appreciate the sport. They didn't pay StubHub fees to rub up against back hair while getting to their seats. The exception might exist for drunken college guys with words spelled out on their bellies, but only provided they're all sufficiently fat and everybody is clear this is a joke.

MAN RULES

If you find yourself in a park on a hot day you must have a stationary place to put your shirt, it should not be tucked into your waste band as you aimlessly power walk. It's hot out, don't make it worse. You don't see cowboys riding horseback with their tops off. If you actually had an active lifestyle you wouldn't need the supplemental sun. This isn't a catalog shoot. If it were, you wouldn't have been hired.

Unless you're playing a pick up games where somebody insists on shirts vs. skins, you're a shirt. Head sweat will fly, arms might get a bit moist, but there's no excuse for rubbing your sweaty back or chest up against another man. If you tried that in the sauna at the gym, you'd be disbarred. Or gang raped, depending on how rough your gym is.

You can never be topless at any time while wearing full-length pants. This goes for anybody over the age of four. If you're a Kennedy rigging a sailboat in the summer in New England for positive press footage, or if you are a genie, you have an exception. Otherwise you look like you're running from the cops. Or from your girlfriend who caught you cheating, and now you wish it were the cops.

When the time comes for you and your buddies to remove your shirts, you shouldn't be the first or last in a group to engage. First leaves you pegged as the guy who loves to shower with the door open and last will make people wonder if you secretly have female breasts. Look at it like trying the brownish ground appetizer at your Albanian friend's house. Let someone else test the waters. Clouds tend to roll in, so does the manager of the convenience store. Keep your shirt on whenever possible.

APPAREL

A Man Doesn't Overdress Or Underdress

People say that clothes make the man, but not any man you'd want to associate with. A man should look at dressing as an annoying necessity and strive to complete his task expeditiously, and blankly, as he would a tetanus shot or visit with his in-laws. Most accomplishments in life demand excellence. With fashion you should be satisfied with a C-plus. Nobody likes the guy who wears the Red Wings jersey to the funeral or the one who shows up to poker night in an ascot. Find some collared shirts and non-jeans pants that fit and fall within a reasonable norm of current style. Buy them in bulk and stock your entire closet like you're Einstein or Seth Brundle from "The Fly".

Formal occasions such as weddings or parole hearings call for a suit. You should own two or three reasonable quality suits. If they're sold in volume or as 2-fers, they're not reasonable quality. A cheap suit signifies a lack of self-respect and imbues you with the look of a car salesman who cheats at Monopoly. Have your suit tailored to fit your body. Women treat you differently in a nice suit. The clothing itself signifies you can be sophisticated, for at least as long as it takes you to return to your hotel to rent porn and eat hot wings.

Only in certain circumstances such as depositions or presidential campaigns will you need to wear entirely ornamental fashion such as a tie. A tie is a decorative accessory that men were conned into wearing long ago to associate themselves with royalty who wore elegant neckwear to hide their goiters. Men don't choose to accessorize. It must be a burden placed upon them by an outside authority. However, the importance of the jacket cannot be undersold. Under no circumstances should you appear at an event in dress or formal clothes without a jacket. This isn't the eighth grade dance. As for formal footwear, you don't need to wear patent leather shoes anymore unless you plan on delivering an impromptu magic act. Simple leather oxfords or brogues look fashionable, provide traction and don't feel like you've shoved your foot into an empty box of Cheerios.

Sweatpants are a divisive issue. Just like there's a difference between a Ferrari and a Kia, sweats can be grouped into various tiers. Running errands on a Sunday in a new pair of track pants is perfectly acceptable. When the sun goes down you should change into something sturdier if you're patronizing pubs or taverns. The bulky gray Haynes with the drawstring and mustard stain should be given to the Salvation Army or destroyed in someone else's garbage disposal. Wearing gym clothes anywhere in public that is not a gymnasium will cause society to judge you as having given up on success. Do tech billionaires get away with dressing like slobs at restaurants? Yes. Follow their lead, once you're a tech billionaire.

Wearing shorts to dinner is fine if you're in Bermuda, or Jimmy Buffett music is playing anywhere over the central sound system. Shorts in the evening generally make you look like you're trying to relive your youth. That holds even if you're still in your youth. If you're on an airplane or attending a cocktail party, put some pants on. There's no reason for a man to presume his legs are attractive to anyone else. If you do so presume, you might as well try heels. They will accentuate your calves.

When worn, shorts should come full to the knee. There should be a zero percent chance of your genitals ever making an appearance. You don't pay by the linear foot; when in doubt buy a size larger. Guys who wear short shorts often find themselves randomly being assaulted by strangers. Violence is never the answer yet in most states there is special legislation protecting the assailants.

A man spends only the amount of time absolutely needed on fashion. It's not important to be the most fashionable male in your professional or social circle. Just don't be the least. Find a happy middle ground from which to understand that the measure of a man will never be his wardrobe. You have more important things to do in this life than find the perfect summer sweater. Yet many of those accomplishments will come easier if you don't resemble the Unabomber. There will be plenty of occasions when entirely alone or with your male friends to whip out the weed t-shirt and tattered college sweats and cover yourself in condiments.

A Man Has No Need for Bling

Jewelry is decorative items favored by women to make them appear prettier. Men have no desire to be pretty. They sure as shit do not wish to sparkle. The very prospect of superficial adornment is futile and lacking a concrete benefit. Jewelry creates hassles at airport security and the threat of being mugged by drug addicts and unemployed journalism majors. It makes you look particularly uninteresting and besides you should be spending that money on a jet ski.

There are very few situations in which it is appropriate for a man to adorn himself with gems or precious metals:

Wedding rings are a notable exception. Every culture has a different explanation as to the origin and significance of the wedding ring, but suffice it to say, you knew it was coming so shut up and wear it. One thing a man does not do is welching on his promises, let alone holy vows. Nor does he create a stink about largely trivial matters. The wedding ring signifies your undying love for your spouse and lets the women at the airport bar know you're either taken or highly sought after depending on your mood.

Championship rings are also acceptable. Be very circumspect as to defining a championship ring. Nobody can deny you won the eighth grade district basketball tournament with grit and determination. That doesn't count. Try an NCAA championship in the least and work your way on up to a Super Bowl title. Keep in mind, championship rings are only acceptable if they were achieved in a real sport. If you have to ask if yours is a real sport, it is not. In short, this champion's exception likely does not apply to you.

Graduating from a four-year college is not ring-worthy. One-third of the U.S. currently does that. So it is as common as leading STDs. Would you wear a ring to mark your HPV? Not even if the contraction story was amazing. Put that oversized Florida State ring back in the sock drawer. When your son is of age you may pass it on to him so that he may look awkward and confused and mumble out a thank you.

Necklaces and bracelets are entirely off limits unless you're a rapper with multiple million confirmed album sales, in which case braided gold by the foot is simply part of your reputation. Unlike the fact you were born in the suburbs and attended private school and studied method drama. If you are at least one-eighth Native American and have slain a shark, bear, or other large non-migratory predator with your bare hands you may take a claw or tooth and wear it as a necklace, preferably leather. This applies only if the beast made the first move on you, not if you went trophy hunting.

Earrings are completely off limits unless you are a Pacific Islander and over 300 pounds. Large Polynesian men can do whatever they want. Failing that you simply look like you're living out all the junior high school fantasies that your mother promptly shot down. The amount of sex you need to have with different beautiful young women to counter the emasculating quality of that diamond stud is massive. So unless you are playing bass in a hit rock band or are a top receiver for the Cowboys, let it go. Substitute English teacher is not the same thing and all the kids you assume think you're cool likely have an unflattering nickname for you.

A man should have no desire to be shiny or fabulous in any manner. The mere mention of those terms in regard to a man spins a voodoo curse diminishing his virility. Whatever you intended to purchase for yourself jewelry wise, save for your current or future female mate. If the thought of a nipple ring has ever crossed your mind, call your parents now and let them know any grandchildren you may have for them in the future will necessarily be adopted.

Men Only Wear Natural Fibers

Under no circumstances should a man put something on his body that is not made entirely of cotton or wool. Men have been wearing nothing but cotton and wool products for centuries both out of necessity and because inherently they understood the emasculation of shiny polymers.

Wool was invented in 5,000 B.C. when some lonely farmer realized that the ewe he was banging was not bothered in the least by the chill winter night, while he was freezing his bare ass off. Men are dominant by nature and wool is a byproduct of this manly dominance. Man saw something weaker than him, with something better than him, so he took it. Not only did he take it, but he did it using the first skill a boy learns when he becomes a man. He shaved it. This makes wool inherently manly.

The only fabric rivaling wool in manliness is cotton. Wool may involve shaving and stealing from the weak but cotton involves grueling physical labor and war. Picking cotton is such hard work that cotton producers had to enslave an entire continent to get the job done. This resulted in the only war ever fought on American soil. Brothers fought each other to the death over cotton. No other wardrobe material has ever caused a war. It came close when rayon became popular in the 1970s, but even that would have been a war about the absence of cotton.

Cotton and wool make manly clothes. This is especially true when it comes to suits. Men have worn suits since the 17th century. No other outfit has been as associated with manliness as a suit. From King Charles to James Bond, great men throughout history have worn suits. That doesn't mean that a man always has to wear a suit, but when he does, he has to do it right. Cheap suits never fit right and are made with manufactured fabrics like polyester. The only thing a polyester suit is good for is making your butt sweat. You know who has sweaty butts? People with nervous butts, and a real man's ass never has to worry.

In some cultures, men do wear silk. But remember that silk is a finery, a desirable delicate fabric for such thing as women's clothing and dresses that they must constantly fuss over as in 'Oh, no, it's silk, that stain will never come out.' A man can't wear a fabric where stains won't come out. That's poor planning. And above all else, men are good planners. In short, stick to natural fibers, primarily cotton and wool, occasionally silk, and once in a great while, mohair.

Men Don't Oblige Fancy Footwear

If it weren't for terrain and current social standards men would walk the earth as hobbits. Men walked around barefoot for centuries with ease. After a few days without shoes, your feet develop enough calluses to scale even the roughest of terra firma. Women wear shoes because they want to look fashionable. Men wear shoes to keep their feet from gangrene.

MAN RULES

Modern society has forced men to adapt to wearing shoes. But, as with all things in his purview, a man stresses function over form. A man's shoe rack should contain no more than four pairs of shoes:

1. A pair of black dress shoes if he works in a bank or for honoring his dead or married comrades.

2. A pair of sneakers for sporting-related activities, poker night, or any other event not involving women.

3. A pair of casual dress shoes for work or dates or restaurants that are not sports bars or fast food.

4. A pair of work boots, earned through actual professional work or more involved home repair projects.

That is it. Men do not wear sandals or flip-flops unless sand is beneath their feet. Men do not need numerous pairs of athletic shoes unless their ticket has been punched to the next Olympic games. You're 30 and you work in accounting; do you need that pair of high tops? Mr. Rogers changed into loafers and a cardigan when he got home. Are you a gray-haired bachelor who plays with puppets? You don't need a colorful array of footwear.

If you find yourself browsing lovely men's patent leather shoes, and they do make them, ask yourself how they might feel while chopping wood or running into a building to save a family of fourteen from a fire. That's how a man thinks. Be ready, pack light, and try not to look like an asshole. The simpler a man keeps his life, the easier it is for masculinity to flow throw his veins.

Skinny Jeans Do Not Belong in a Man's Drawer

Jeans were invented so that men would no longer have to think about what to wear beneath their waist. The savings in productivity has allowed men to construct magnificent dams, great bridges, and converted basement rec rooms. A woman may ponder the type of slacks that best complements her figure. A man finds the smallest waist size denim pants he can pull up without suffering a hernia and buys two pairs to last through the next millennium.

Men don't seek extreme comfort in their pants, nor do they covet style. Jeans are a tool very much the same as a wrench or a hammer. Nobody runs into Home Depot looking for a screwdriver that works well with the color of his laundry room. Nor should you be looking to make a fashion statement with your jeans. This most definitely includes pretending you accidentally bought tailored "skinny jeans".

Whether you are rail thin or morbidly obese or somewhere in the middle, a man does not wear tightly cut pants ever. Whatever skinny jeans can do regular jeans can do and without making you look like a marionette. You are not the ironic hipster king of Williamsburg or Austin or Silverlake. You do not sit on a throne of old PBR cans discussing whether 180 gram vinyl records are worth the price. If you are, wear pants so tight your femoral arteries collapse. You're easily replaceable in the herd.

Cutting jeans so tight they inform the public of your religious upbringing is downright unpatriotic. Is there any more American and manly a piece of clothing than blue jeans? Men have worn a pair of Levis in the Old West, mining for coal in Pennsylvania, building cars in Detroit, and riding Harleys across country in the 60's. The fit of these jeans was determined by use. When you first got a pair of jeans they used to be stiff and rough like sandpaper. With continued wear, time, and exposure to the elements they would soften and conform to your body comfortably, and any tightness was caused by your own girth, not design. You earned the comfort; it didn't come thanks to stone washing.

Regarding color: they are called blue jeans. They aren't red jeans, green jeans, black jeans, and certainly not white jeans. Can you imagine Marlon Brando in "The Wild Ones" wearing white jeans? His own biker gang would have shanked him. No jury in the world would have found them guilty. Men wear clothes that fit them comfortably enough. Chicks wear form-fitting clothes to show off their curves to attract a male mate. Men are instinctually visual. Are you trying to attract a male mate? Then why must we see how hard you've been working on your calves? Wear jeans that allude to, but don't expressly reveal, your undercarriage. Let your woman be pleasantly surprised when you drop your not-tight blue jeans, like that Christmas when she got that vibrating handheld showerhead.

Men Don't Wear New Team Sports Gear in Season

Wearing fresh team apparel during the season is a surefire way to piss off every decent man on the planet. Once the season starts, only the nastiest, grungiest, most veteran articles of sports team clothing should touch a man's body. New gear is strictly for wearing out in the off-season when the bandwagon fans have long since packed away their brand new purchases.

This rule is about more than just sports, it's about values. What men value most in a sports fan is loyalty and dedication. The biggest indicator of a man's loyalty and dedication to his team is the number of years he has been a fan. The longer a man has bled for a team, the more loyal and dedicated he is, which makes him a better fan, and a better man.

Simply being a fan for a long time in your heart of hearts is not enough; you have to be able to prove it. As a gender, men are notorious braggarts and exaggerators. Every man wants to be the best, but some settle for just pretending to be the best. A man is just as likely to embellish how long he has supported his team as he is likely to embellish his penis size. The difference is, you can't whip out your penis in a bar to prove you have a big dick, but you can sport team-colored Zubaz to prove you've been a fan since back in the 80s.

That clearly does not mean searching for vintage sports gear on eBay. Fandom is not bought; it is passed down from generation to generation. If you or someone close to you did not originally own it, it is not going to fly. Whether it is your grandma's homemade California Angels sweater, or your friend's dad's brother's Larry Bird jersey, if you cannot trace the history back more than a decade, you should not be wearing it during the season.

The importance of this rule, as well as the severity of the punishment for violation, increases exponentially as your team is doing well. If the Steelers make it to the playoffs and you are suddenly decked out in fresh black and gold, you are likely to get your butt kicked. If the Cubs are playing in the World Series and the only gear you have has "Chicago Cubs National League Champs" from the same post-season written in fresh letters across the chest, you might just start a riot. And if you die in that riot, nobody will come to your funeral.

Panic not. All that money you spent on new gear will not go to waste. It is perfectly acceptable to wear in the off-season. Real men support their team year round. Whether brand new or decades old, there is nothing manlier than a hockey jersey worn in August. And if you are still dead set on wearing your new purchases during the season, that is fine, you'll just have to wait another ten years. Don't label yourself a heretic. Men don't fight the rules they themselves concocted.

FRIENDS AND FAMILY

So Your Sibling Had a Baby

Being an uncle is one of life's great pleasures. Your brother or sister's children will worship you simply for the moniker. The title bestows upon the bearer fantastical skills and a backstory involving bear wrestling and motorcycle stunt work. None of this need be remotely true. When you're five the school principal seems like a feudal warlord, as opposed to a bureaucrat with a broken marriage and an addiction to nasal spray.

As an uncle you're coming into a child's life with a huge perception advantage. You're a de facto rebel to whom the rules of their oppressive parents hold no authority. When you start purchasing their affection in the form of toys their parents would never allow, they are prepared to sign a billion-year Sea Org contract to be your minions. Seal the deal by allowing them to drink maple syrup out of the bottle and watch movies with ratings that will make them heroes among their tiny friends.

Your nieces and nephews aren't your kids, but you have a familial obligation to maintain a strong relationship with them. It's the reasonable extension of the blood ties a man holds with his siblings. You're not their first line of support, but you are in line. Think of yourself as a parental stand-in. By proxy you hold dominion over these little people. If your niece is pelting your ears with Miley Cyrus covers you can freely tell her to shut it without fear of dismissal. The same cannot be said for the children of your friends. Your friends expect you to blindly witness the apoplectic tantrums of their son or daughter and clap like a seal. Were you to chide or discipline a friend's child, they would consider you way out of bounds. If you do the same to a niece of nephew, you'll be asked to take the kids as often as you are available.

With this inherent privilege comes responsibility, first and foremost among them being to honor their special occasions with cool gifts. Presents are only for your own direct kin, not for your friends' kids. In fact, it's weird and should be discouraged. A man only buys gifts for family members or women he's trying to coax into an intimate relationship. If you've circled your buddy's daughter's birthday on your calendar prepare to stop being invited to the barbecues.

Typically, you can skip the first year. Infants are oblivious to the world and new parents have been inundated with a lot of baby crap. To simplify your life, find a gift theme for your niece or nephew related to a specific interest (coin collection, baseball cards, fishing tackle, musical instruments) and stick with it. There will come an age at which they share with you they were never into fishing like you thought. Don't take this as a sign of your failure so much as a sign that you may now start buying them Amazon gift cards without seeming lazy.

Once your niece or nephew reaches young adult status, they should be able to confide in you as a consigliore. Barring something truly dangerous, you shouldn't tattle to their parents. A child needs one adult in their life to validate their decisions without value judgment or recrimination. Since they nixed woodshop in middle schools, these adult confidants are getting harder and harder to find. Your niece or nephew is almost certainly up to something stupid. Smile and give them reassuring thumbs up. Never put anything in writing or leave any recorded messages. You're going to want plausible deniability when they break their arm from the dangerous skateboard jump you assured them was legendary.

After the formative years it's smooth sailing. They'll probably bother you to buy them booze or pot at some point. Politely refuse but give them some alternative ideas that won't get them arrested. Soon they'll be off to the college you in no way had to pay for and will be old enough to take to ball games or shoot pool with at the local dive. A man understands that family comes first, both his own brood and his extended family. The clan is the basic building block of a secure and caring community and a healthy nation at large. It will all be worthwhile someday when your twenty-something niece or nephew invites you to their wild backyard party filled with co-eds. No, you're not attending. But it was an honor all the same.

A Man Never Speaks Ill of a Friend's Girl

There are times in your life where you will be madly intoxicated with a truly horrible woman. It's a rite of passage and nearly impossible to avoid as you make your way through the lesson-learning phases of your life. The same mistakes will occur to your friends. Golden Rule this carefully and treat buddies in these circumstances as you would wish to be treated yourself. Every man has at one time dated a severely disturbed woman who quite coincidentally has a fixation on providing oral sex and suggests she'd like to get her attractive friends into the bedroom with you. Your friends said nothing to you at the time because they assumed you had it under control. They were also secretly jealous. If your friend starts bringing around a girl who reads star charts and carries a squirrel in a small mesh bag, keep your opinions to yourself. Even if you heard from the last guy she dated that she did very weird things with winter gourds, this isn't junior high school. You shouldn't go around repeating stories you heard from the guy who rotates your tires. A man keeps his opinions about his friend's girlfriends to himself. Your buddy isn't perfect, and if this woman is attracted to him she's probably not either. He's a grown man. He's getting something out of this relationship.

We've all had a friend deeply involved with a horrible woman. Most women are not horrible. Most women are amazing. Due to statistical anomalies, horrible women will still occur to the vast number of your male acquaintances. It is clear to everyone that this woman is entirely wrong for him, let alone any sentient being on two feet. Sometimes you are asked to stand up on the altar with him as he legally binds himself to her for a lifetime, or at least several years, of suffering.

Your options are dramatically limited. You can't tell a buddy, "Dude, don't marry this succubus". He obviously doesn't see her the same way you do and you've far exceeded your lawful role as a male friend. You will inexorably ruin your friendship and in no way prevent him undertaking his current path of mistaken lust and forlorn kinship. Trust that your friend is smart enough to eventually come around. It's best to let him find out for himself that the love of his life is sucking out his soul piece by piece.

When the inevitable happens and they break-up, your first instinct may be to celebrate. Suppress this impulse. Certainly you are happy that your buddy is free of her manhood-crushing claws and on a purely selfish level that you never have to interact with this shrill she-demon ever again. But if your other friend starts calling her names and bitching about her, don't join in. It's a trap. Simply pronounce, "Dude, I'm with you." and shake your head in a general pantomime of sympathetic understanding.

Quite often the first breakup never holds. Many a male friendship has ended with premature ex-girlfriend or wife bashing. The most dangerous time is in the immediate aftermath of a break-up. It is a massive mistake to verbally tear into a friend's recent ex. What happens when she moves back in a month? He won't soon forget that you called her a "donkey blowing hose beast", and neither will she. Knowing you bad-mouthed her, she is going encourage him to stay away from you. If you don't believe your friends are as poorly skilled as yourself when picking out a great woman in their formative years, you're wrong.

Almost all men falter in this regard and suffer a few past heartbreaks and bumps in the road. Women have a much stronger sense of intuition than men. Also, men think with their penis. This is why nature never constructed monogamous relationships or equipped men to be gifted in creating them. Tree houses and carburetors are much easier.

A Man Lends A Hand in Moderation

Men are independent creatures, but not isolated beings. Men construct social circles to compensate for those things they can't do entirely for themselves. For instance, when you need to unload some lumber without throwing your back out again, that's what friends are for. It reveals a lack of class to keep score amongst friends as to who's doing more favors, but certainly a rough tally is in order. Everyone hates the guy who has his friends refurbish his two-story home, paying them in nine bucks worth of pizza and beer, and then is then mysteriously busy when you need someone to hold the other side of a tape measure. Don't be the needy guy or the guy who's first on everybody's list for assistance. Find a sustainable middle.

If you do two favors in a row for a buddy, skip the third and wait until you need help moving your anvil collection. You'll see who your real friends are. Learn to say no and think of some go-to excuses. If it gets around that you're the guy who's chomping at the bit to pull landscaping duty, your phone will never stop ringing. That request line traffic doubles if you choose to drive a pick-up. You have no idea how many couches people are buying, at least two per week.

Establish some boundaries. If you and your buddy find it mutually beneficial to drive each other to the airport that's fine, although past college you should be able to transport yourself within the borders of your own city. Uber is fifteen bucks and the payment on the card isn't due for a month. Maintain a similar rule when it comes to moving. Imagine how much you're dreading your own move and realize you're bringing other people into your own personal hell. Once you're working full-time you should be able to pay some ex-cons to move a bureau. If you're relocating due to a death or conflagration, or if everything you own fits into a Kia, that's the time to call the friend network.

A man might ask his friends for help with a task, never a job. Jump-starting a car is a task; scrubbing toilets is a job. A task is measured in minutes. A job is measured in hours. A man doesn't work half a day without getting paid. If your buddy is a certified carpenter and spends ninety minutes taking a hand plane to your cabinets, burgers and a couple brews on you should be fine. Longer than that, cold hard cash off the books.

You should not be hesitant to hire your responsible friends for work you'd otherwise hire a stranger to perform, but you have to pay them. If money is short or comes off as too awkward, bartering is a manly substitute. Bartering existed as a currency among men long before there were coins or printed bills. If you're a mechanic and your buddy is a roofer, he does your roof and you make that P.O.S. dripping oil in his driveway turnover once more. Most of your friends should have something to offer. Avoid the friend who's offering drugs in exchange for assistance. Outside of the moral ramifications, once he's on probation his value will run out and he'll have nothing left to barter.

You and a buddy may have a tacit agreement to provide free labor to each other in the name of saving money. There's nothing wrong with such an arrangement if finances are tight, yet if you find this equitable heading into your thirties it's time to refocus your career path. A man treasures his independence not only for what it means for him, but for what it means to those around him who no longer need to support him. It took a village. Now the village is ready to be done with you. A strong signal of this matriculation is the ability to leave the favor system behind and move on to a cash economy where you are creating jobs for others and your friends aren't scared to answer your calls.

A Man Supports His Friends

You can tell a lot about a man by the company he keeps. Children have all sorts of friends of disparate character. The biggest jerk always has the best video games. God does that to be cruel. By the time you've finished college you've ideally weeded out the neighborhood kid who huffs paint and finds it amusing to be aimless. A man should value his friends because they care about his well being, have his back in any altercation, and above all else will listen to his boring stories and feign amusement. Your friends have been there for you. You need to repay that blessing by being a solid friend in return. That doesn't mean deep involvement in your buddy's business. What separates men from women in friendship bonds is a man's understanding that you're there for support, not proactive intervention.

If your friend is hitting the bottle too hard or mulling a career change to carnival barker you need to keep them on their rocker without pushing too hard. Stubbornness is a survival mechanism for men. They are prone to doubling down on their bets to prove a point. If you can't assist them in bettering their current situation, don't harp on how unpleasant it is. If you feel a need to intervene, don't get together a group of friends and relatives and ruin what he thought was going to be an hour of Game of Thrones and a few beers with you. One-on-one is how a man confronts another man. People don't change unless they have the internal desire to change. Lay off the platitudes and take them to a ballgame. Your life isn't perfect either, Captain America.

You should limit the instances in which you lend money to friends. Not because of the financial strain upon yourself, but because of the awkward position you've now put them in with your generosity. It's embarrassing for a man to have to call upon his friends for something even more substantial than moving help. The feelings of humiliation prevent it from being a routine event. If you lend money to a friend, be prepared to not get it back. They may be borrowing from several people at once or end up in prison next week. Don't lend anything you can't afford to lose. One time should be your limit. Twice and you start becoming the Monopoly bank rather than a friend. Whatever was there in terms of fraternal closeness will now fade into awkward feelings and calls going direct to voicemail.

Men make friends for life. Not just because of their tendency toward fierce loyalty, but because men are generally not inclined to keep making new ones. Men don't love to socialize. When you form a bond in high school, that friendship often carries to your grave. You don't want to be forty and looking for new best friends. It's tiresome and much like middle aged dating, the good ones are already taken. A man's richness is measured in his family and friends. Be thought of in high regard by a number of other good and decent men and you will be a wealthy man.

A Man Carefully Evaluates His Legacy Friendships

You'll make numerous friends for life in your K-12 years. You'll also meet a few guys who end up manufacturing drugs behind a convenience store. Men have a difficult time differentiating between friends and cohorts. Friends are people you will someday go halfsies with on season tickets and trust with your children's care. Cohorts are people you assemble for an intoxicated break-in to the County pool for late night skinny dipping with a couple girls you met visiting from Oregon. Once you're eighteen, don't feel obligated to hot box with the old varsity defensive line. People have different paths in life. For some it leads straight to washing dishes at an old folks' home. You have bigger plans, including things you need to get done tomorrow before two in the afternoon.

You should make an effort to gather with the guys you grew up with at least once a year. A trip to Vegas is ideal but a bar crawl of your hometown works just as well. You need to spend some time with a group of people who absolutely do not care about your feelings of self-worth. They'll be honest that you look like a tool in grey jeans and that it's time to give up that side gig as a street puppeteer. They have your best interest at heart.

No matter how many bodies you and the boys buried back in the day, you need to get out there and expand your social circle. True, half the guys you meet as an adult just want to be your real estate agent or screw your girlfriend, but it's important to try. Pal around exclusively with your high school buddies and all your conversations eventually turn to who nailed that really long keg stand and which among you was the first to get with that hot

THE BEGINNER'S GUIDE TO MANHOOD

cheerleader chick who some years of perspective will force you all to admit wasn't all that hot. The insider references become tiresome to other people around. Your behavior by nature becomes exceedingly juvenile and women just assume you sleep in a racecar bed.

Mathematically speaking a very small percentage of your high school buddies have the chops to be the coolest guy in the room. Insulate yourself and you're missing out on a lot of new friends with much fresher stories and probably more interesting backgrounds that are less likely to fist fight strangers. A man should always be moving up, yet never forget where he came from. For that reason, you need to thin the herd and then treat the surviving members like brothers.

Men Most Cautiously Mix Business With Friend and Family

Going into business with a personal friend has its risk and benefits. For every Smith & Wesson or Harley-Davidson there are ten guys suing former drinking buddies for skimming the quarters from their do it yourself car wash. Consider how much you value your friendship, because there's a strong chance it will end the moment you vote your buddy off the board because he's convinced he has the ability to summon the rain. Baskin stabbed Robbins to death with a sugar cone; little known fact. Most people agreed Robbins was a prick.

If you are starting a business from the ground up, make sure everything is split evenly. Resentment brews anytime someone receivers a larger cut. Your company could pull in a billion dollars a year and if one partner were fifty bucks short a drunken blowout would ensue. Men are innately petty when it comes to the fruits of their labor. It's related to survival. Don't touch my stuff being a very normal, though not high-minded instinct. Men also engage routinely in first-person bias that causes both men in a partnership to believe they complete ninety-percent of the work. This makes almost all partnerships inherently fraught with peril. A man doesn't shy away from peril, nor does he embrace it as he might a buxom woman.

As with monetary splits goes decision making among partners. Everything must be mutual. Men are prideful to a fault. Once a guy feels his voice isn't being heard he starts donning infrared goggles and sabotaging the forklifts. It doesn't make sense but presumably the apes in the zoo would do the same if they had jobs or access to equipment.

Size up your friend before entering any arrangement. Don't consider his value to you as the guy with that stupid cool American vintage roadster; measure him only as a future business partner. You can walk away right now and nobody's feelings will be hurt. Does he frequently get loaded on tequila and sleep until noon? Did he quit college to hunt for stolen treasure and end up with malaria? When there's a bowl of mints out at the restaurant does he empty it into his cargo pockets, even the ones that aren't individually wrapped and often contain trace amounts of human urine? As with a romantic relationship, there are almost always warning signs before entering toxic business relationships. Look at his history. He can still be your buddy if he beat a man nearly to death at work. He had his reasons. You wouldn't ever want to be on the receiving end to find out. People don't really change. This is life, not the movies.

The same lessons of business partnership apply when potentially employing a friend. Whether he'd be stocking a warehouse, maintaining your faux rock pool or plowing your driveway, avoid hiring the guy you went to high school with who has multiple arrests. Everybody deserves one without being judged. Restraining orders are also typically an indicator of character deficit. Almost certainly he's going to perform poorly, you're going to get rid of him, and that's going to end the friendship. Compounding matters, he now has nothing to do all day but sit at the local pub and talk trash about you to every other loser in town, who will in turn spread those rumors like gospel. How did he make your pool turn into a burning lake of fire? If only he had applied so much energy to the original job of cleaning.

You can never go wrong by separating business from friendship. The same certainly goes for family. Though you can also create hurt feelings by turning down opportunities from within your social circle. Though a man recognizes that when feelings get hurt in the course of choosing the higher road, those feelings are to be largely discounted. Ben & Jerry have lasted thirty-seven years of edging America

MAN THINGS

Your Car Is Not a Dress Up Doll

Men like the power and thrill of the internal combustion engine and things that go vroom. Give a small boy a toy car and he will instinctively echo the sound of an engine emitting carbon into the atmosphere in the name of speed. Cars are a pleasure, but possessing a car is not the same as having a girlfriend or owning a dog. A man doesn't let himself get attached to inanimate objects. You shouldn't drive anything you can't walk away from if you spot the heat around the corner.

Accessorizing your vehicle is no more than dressing up a doll. Men don't play with dolls. The very term 'accessory' connotes something not of fundamental importance. Men have no time for frills, not when there are mouths to feed and men to kill in foreign lands. If you apply a spoiler you bought from Hobby Lobby with a calking gun to a Honda Civic, it's still a Honda Civic. Men know better than to imagine wind differential matters when you're doing thirty in a residential area.

A bumper sticker is worse than a spoiler. A bumper sticker signifies to the world that you don't write your own jokes. A bumper stick declares that an issue is so goddamn important to you that you insist on sharing it with complete strangers in traffic behind you. How much do you really care about rent control or locally grown produce? Not that much. Not if you're a man.

Windshield decals signify you're a fan of smoking meth in your garage. A sticker featuring any band is a green light for the cops to pull you over and tell you they don't want to catch you again in these parts, you dirty hippy. Is that marijuana joint in your dash-mounted mini gumball machine? Stop decorating.

A man's keychain should be functional. A bottle opener or nail clippers are fine because a multipurpose tool gets you one step closer to heaven. A purely decorative key chain tells the world that you went to Coachella. It also tells the world you're not a man. In similar fashion, an air-freshener tells the world your car stinks. Why does your car stink and why are you trying to cover it up like a Frenchman with cologne? "Frenchman" is an oxymoron.

Seat covers are for grandmothers. Did you raise three kids alone during the war? You did not. Lose the seat covers.

There should never be liquidation sale speakers where your luggage is supposed to go. If your trunk resembles Angus Young's Marshall stacks, you are liable to be mistaken for a gang member. Men are too savvy to die in street shootouts.

The more crap you've got loaded in your car the more there is to entice drug-addicted drifters to break in and steal your cigarette lighter-powered ice cream maker. A man drives because he has places to be. Maybe there's a cow stuck in a ravine out on the North Forty. Does the cow care that you have a hula dancer on your dashboard? That's a trick question. A cow is female. Of course she does. Keep it simple.

Men Own Dogs

A man is not a zookeeper. He owns one, maybe two, non-human creatures. They are dogs.

In all the animal kingdom, canines have the greatest affinity with the males of the human species. Dogs have a very streamlined list of needs. They know not to defecate where they eat. All other rules are secondary. Their loyalty is unmatched. The same cannot be said for felines or birds, which have been known to point out the location of the jewelry box to intruders.

You might consider reptiles. In which case it's wise to remember the axiom: nobody likes the guy with the snake. His house smells of rotting flesh and he's a little too excited to watch mice swallowed alive. He likes Eastern European horror films and gives off the impression that he consumes cheap drugs. For these reasons, he repels women with the force of a fire hose. A tropical fish aquarium might seem appealing to you, if you enjoy things that swim in their own waste. Don't allow a pet into your home that will one day exit your abode through the toilet.

A man chooses his dog wisely. A dog is ten-to-fifteen years of your life, less if you live near coyotes. Nobody takes a man with a small dog seriously. It's not as entirely corresponding to penis size as is a man's choice in cars, but it's certainly close. For the same reason, you should not overcompensate obviously with a rambunctious German Shepherd in your studio apartment. Dogs were meant to hunt, not watch reruns on TV Land. If your dog can't regularly go outdoors you shouldn't own it. It's not fair to the animal or the neighbors downstairs who have to overhear Buddy using his head as a battering ram to break down the door in a continuous attempt at a prison break.

Pit bull owners will announce to anyone who will listen that the breed is misunderstood and not prone to vicious attack even as their dog mauls the neighbor kid in the next room. Along with Rottweilers and Dobermans you need to understand there's significant risk with dogs featured in Animal Control most-wanted lists, and that you don't have Bluebeard's hoard in your sub-basement needing protection. You don't associate with ex-cons for a reason, so avoid any dog that you're reasonably suspicious could put a bullet in someone.

Mutts are the best dogs. One look at Prince Charles should cement this. That Great Dane might look reasonably cool on the shelf at the puppy mill but by the time you get it home it will need a visit to the chiropractor and titanium hip joint. Your finances will soon be in shambles and you'll have to mortgage the house. Picking up six-pound piles of crap twice daily is no way to live. All things in moderation, including non-speaking, non-working, hair-covered members of your extended family.

Your dog can go with you to the park, beach, or to the cabin but it does not belong in the Denny's or the gym sauna or in economy on a transcontinental airline flight. If you need a therapeutic animal in order to keep you from fits of anxiety or rage in a pressurized cabin at 35,000 feet, you should probably take the train.

A Man Keeps His Man Cave Simple

A Man Cave is a sanctuary from the hustle and bustle of the rest of the house. A fortress of solitude where a dirty sock momentarily left on the floor will not trigger a Shawshank lockdown. Farting the theme song to Sanford and Son at the dinner table remains widely frowned upon. In the Man Cave it's rewarded with a decent score from even the East German judge. It is a man's inalienable right to trick out his garage, basement, or a makeshift ice fishing shack on the front lawn in the manner of an impulsive seventh grader who won the Powerball.

The décor should be more James Bond than Buffalo Bill. A Kegerator, gaming setup, pool table and dartboard are standard issue. Downward-facing-dog Penthouse pinups and blowup dolls are flying to close to the sun. Just because it's a Man Cave doesn't mean women should reach reflexively for the pepper spray in their purse upon entering. Get a complete set of decent poker chips, because there's nothing more pathetic than a group of dudes anteing up with checkers and different types of Ritz Crackers. Respect your own property. Nobody cares if you want to watch retro porn while smoking a pipe in a Broncos onesie and eating lasagna sans fork, just don't be a slob about it. Don't leave leftover pizza lying around and extricate your empty beer bottles to the blue bin. A real man recycles. After your teen masculine apprentice years, there's nothing to be gained by leaving your empty bottles around to show off your drinking bona fides. The scoring system changes after college.

Invest in a good couch. You're going to be spending 99 percent of your Man Cave time tucked into its cushions. A retread from Goodwill signals to the rest of the world that you will park yourself literally anywhere. A king has his thrown and a regal divan. You're not a king; you're also not a pauper. Find the acceptable middle. Preferably acquire something stain-repellent and a darker color to obscure obvious signs of red sauce. Women are born with the ability to know when they're seated on a dirty couch, even if the dirt is not visible to the naked eye. Dogs can smell cancer. It's based on the same principle. Couches do need steam cleaning. Once a year is fine if you're not abusive. More may be needed if there was a curry accident during your Diwali celebration.

A man should never get too extravagant or be too comfortable in life. Keep it simple. Yard sales kill an entire Saturday and serve as a reminder you never needed that ornamental tilapia. The optimal term is "cave". The Jacuzzi and hyperbaric chamber are overkill. You're looking for a comfortable place to drink and smoke cigars with your buddies under the pretense you've all become huge fans of the Canadian Football League. The vast majority of the conversation that takes place in the Man Cave will be complete bullshit, but without a woman present, it will be duly accepted. That's why you took the extra work to pay for the Man Cave.

The average hard-working man needs about ten hours a week to be completely useless, most of which will ultimately be spent on the weekends.

With minimal effort he can fulfill his dream of scratching his balls uninterrupted without having to explain the plot of the Matrix again. The Man Cave is where dreams come true. Don't overthink it or elevate it to the top three most important elements of your life. It's not an accomplishment. It's a thing.

COMMUNICATIONS

Emoticons Are Emotional Icons for Which Men Have No Use

All technological revolutions have disrupted the customs of men and the ease of masculinity. When automobiles offered men a relatively fast and reliable means of transport, they also removed them from their horses where they had been seated as men for countless generations. So men built much cooler faster cars and raced them. Manufacturers built completely unnecessary muscle cars for men to signal their manhood among their community and clan.

The digital revolution has been an outright assault on masculinity like perhaps no wave of technology before. The Internet has negated the need for numerous male chores and interactions and, in a very sinister manner, sought to gender neutralize its virtual universe. A prime example of this emasculating tool is the emoticon. Emoticons or emojis are a form of textual message, typically used by bored teenage girls, composed of characters and symbols in order to textually express an emotion. The most commonly used emoticon is the smiley face. This is pointless for men to employ, because men don't naturally smile. They may fake a smile to provide for custom or politeness, but they don't mean it. Men are universally aware of danger and it's impossible to smile when you're in danger.

Emoticons naturally imply emotions. Men do not have emotions and if they did on occasion they would never feel the need to show them. Men hide their emotions, burying them deep enough that only years of psychotherapy could ever come close to exposing them. And that psychotherapy would obviously only be done against their will in a camp or prison of some kind. Men do not need symbols that express emotions in a text or email. If anything, men could benefit from something that helps them hide their emotions. Like a picture of a yellow face that revealed how empty its soul was on the inside. Try sending that out to your text buddies with an LOL chaser. You can't, it's too real.

Everything a man has to communicate can be done so without the use of emoticons. In fact, men should never type anything but the twenty-six letters of the alphabet. Anything other than A through Z and a comma, period, or question marks have no place in a message from a man. Emoticons are decoration. The last time you decorated was to support the girl on the prom committee you thought might let you into her pants. And, she didn't, did she? Nope, 250 balloons orally inflated and you couldn't even get to second base. There's your lesson in decoration. Quit using emoticons.

Greet People Like You're A Head of State

Almost daily a man is forced to shake hands with another man. This doesn't even factor in hugs, fist bumps, bows, high fives, or in some parts of Canada, half nelsons while eating deer jerky as a basic form of greeting. Often times this leads to awkward displays of unintelligible sign language between the two parties or the ever-awkward mismatched greeting between parties.

Be on your toes. Like a great linebacker, you see what the offense is providing and quickly adapt. If some guy with a neck tattoo extends his hand for a fist bump, quickly acclimate. Don't grab onto it like you're opening a twenty-foot chamber door in Hogwarts.

You cannot go wrong in any situation with the traditional American white guy handshake. As a visual aid, just watch any Kevin Spacey movie. Upon hearing the first hundredth of a syllable of someone's name, robotically stick your arm out at a 70-degree angle, smile, grab their hand and give it a quick down, up, down. Then immediately let go as if the other man is leper. In Olympic skiing, an extra half-second and you are firmly a loser. The same rules apply here.

Your grip should be firm but you're not trying to prove anything. Men signify their strength in tire changing speed or abundance of charcoal briquettes, not by crippling an unsuspecting calligrapher. Your grip shouldn't crush one of those toy balsa wood planes; merely insure it won't fly straight. Nobody likes a weak wet noodle handshake, it signifies that the man has no morals, which explains why he overcooks his rigatoni.

The most common handshake audible is flawlessly transitioning into what is known as the Brother Handshake. This entails an overhanded clasp with simultaneous back pat. You can spot this one a mile away by the cocked elbow, slight shoulder hunch, and extended thumb. In the horrifying event that you've already gone in for your standard handshake don't panic, it's a simple transition. Rotate your hand over mid shake and pretend you and the other guy attended a boarding school in the Northeast and you do this every week at the Skull and Bones meeting.

Some guys like to bring it in for a hug. This is not to be confused with an embrace. Embraces are a sign of intimacy. Men do not embrace other men outside of immediate family members and only then during decades-long reunions or funerals. For the collegial hug simply bump bellies with the guy and pat his back three or four times like you're putting out a chemical fire. High fives are acceptable only at sporting events amongst strangers or a group setting in which one guy makes another one cry about Monopoly. Don't be the guy who hugs. But don't be the guy who recoils like a sexual assault victim when your friend who grew up with many sisters leans towards hugging. If you're hugging guys you don't know very well, you probably need a girlfriend as everybody who knows you has been telling you for some time.

Greeting women is far more complicated and fraught with embarrassing miscues. When greeting women there are two options. A quick exceedingly gentle handshake or a gentle hug applied with the same force you would use for lifting something large, round, and delicate, like a glass beach ball. The keyword is gentle. Hugging is in a woman's nature. It makes them feel less alone in the universe. Men's greatest desire is to be alone in the universe, or at least their apartment, so a man can never fully appreciate the hug. Arch your ass out like you're Phil Jackson calling the triangle and pretend you're at the seventh grade dance for three seconds. Establish trust as with a feral animal. If you want to break that trust at a later date, that's up to you.

A man only has one chance to make a first impression, sometimes three or four if he associates with a lot of alcoholics. Pick a greeting strategy that works and stick with it. You've seen what happens to the Browns when they adopt a brand new offense every single season. Walking into a room with a reflexive plan calms your social nerves and makes everyone you meet much more comfortable as well. Keep it simple and you'll be calmly talking trash about your new acquaintance at a reasonable distance in no time.

Men Are Not Politically Correct, Nor Are They Belligerent Assholes

A man should not parse his words. Be direct. If you haven't considered your words carefully, why are you speaking? Straightforward speech should not be confused with curtness or generally being a jerk. When your girlfriend asks if she could stand to lose five pounds you don't reply in the affirmative and exit the room. Insensitivity is not a virtue. Espousing your ardent views on social issues of the day to an entire barbecue doesn't mean you're telling it like it is. It means nobody likes you and you're cooking your own burger next Fourth of July. There are appropriate forums for ranting. The public square has grown to an exponential number of easily accessed outlets in the digital age.

While not compromising his moral backbone, a man's speech should reflect the modernity of his times. We can all agree it's a good thing people aren't still telling their Negro to go fetch their golf clubs. The words reflect a shift in culture. The appropriate terminology for describing Native Americans has changed countless times through the years. You could view this as asinine or ask yourself why you care in the first place. If ten members of the Seminole tribe find the term Redskins offensive, what is the principle with which you're fighting to keep the team name? Is the downside really the downfall of Western Civilization or is it likely more so that you'll need to buy a new sweatshirt? A boy engages in every fight. A man picks his battles. A man today should not speak the same as he did during the Great Depression. We've come a long way in dentistry and have automatic transmissions. Evolving is not the same as selling out.

On the flipside, there are people who will abuse your geniality. They'll correct your every word and inform you that it's now a felony to refer to people from Seattle as Washingtonians. The self-righteous have little understanding that the majority of people dislike them every bit as much as the guy expressing World War I-era views on ethnicity at the barbecue.

Political correctness is inherently unmanly. It implies that there are numerous concerns with statements more important than the truth. A man should politely ignore people offended by his speech due entirely to personal beliefs. In contrast, you should consider the thoughts of people with a personal attachment to an issue to which you're commenting. What Gwen the Barista has to say about the appropriate nomenclature for people bound to wheelchairs can be politely ignored. What a paraplegic has to say on the same issue should be considered with respect. A man never feels threatened by making reasonable compromise with those generally disenfranchised or down on their luck

There's a general confusion between sticking up for the rights of the downtrodden and merely being hypersensitive regarding the free expression of others. Sticking up for those who need assistance is a masculine trait.

Wholesale policing of other people's verbiage makes people want to punch you and deservedly so. There may be cases where speech is particularly egregious or hate-filled and should be called out, though never shut down. Your humanity lies in your ability to judge on a case-by-case basis. Linear thinking is an overt signal of lack of intelligence. A man is ever intelligent or at least faking it as best possible. Lead by example. Shouting down idiots has never once worked.

A Man Keeps His Political Opinions to Tight Circles

Discussing politics in today's society carries zero rewards. The people you're arguing with are as lightly informed and highly prejudiced as you are and that poses a serious problem. The chances you will sway another grown individual to view the world through the lens of your same political philosophy within the space of a coffee house rant is approximately nil. The fervency with which people express their views on how to make the world a better place is invariably inversely proportional to their actual hands-on efforts to achieve that same outcome. Mother Theresa would not have been routinely updating her Facebook status with partisan memes. You haven't earned the privilege to make stump speeches to strangers at your nephew's fifth birthday party. You're not a freshman in college anymore. When you're young, political argumentation is just another form of masturbation designed to hold you over until the real world arrives and your time begins to carry an appraisable value.

A man does not initiate political debate because he does not seek to add more fruitless drama to his life. As to incoming discussions, he must learn how to deflect. You should be prepared for those moments when your friend's uncle mentions aloud that people who didn't quite understand trigonometry should be euthanized to save money on healthcare. You have two options. Pretend you didn't hear it and start a new conversation or spend the next three hours engaged in an activity as productive as a freeway car chase from police helicopters. At least the car chase has some action.

If you happen to voice your belief that homeless people should be discouraged from crapping on your lawn, someone in the room will become deeply offended and instinctually compare you to Hitler. As a man, you understand that "being offended" is not a worthwhile emotional state. But we live in a culture where many people confuse self-esteem with expressing offense. There are no masculinity points for defending a political position. It's entirely subjective. This is why men are drawn to sports. A finite, objective score determines victories. Arguing as to whether the Cowboys or Redskins played a better game is moot given that one team won and one team lost. When in social or professional company, gauge your surroundings and err on the side of caution as to engaging in political discourse. Proclaiming that chunky is better than creamy carries very little risk. A man picks his battles wisely and never over nothing.

There will be times in a political discussion when somebody not only expresses their opinion, but lists off factual information that you are quite certain are incorrect. This is the time to call upon the saintly restraint of your ancestors. Rather than launch into a senselessly long battle of data sourcing, simply employ the disarming phrase, "Are you sure about that?" Your innocuous but suggestive inquiry along with a mild grin will encourage everybody to once more discuss the weather.

If you hear something so horrendously off base that your wife is forming a closed fist go ahead and scratch the record. But understand that calling out the guy whose pool you're in means he'll be deleting your name from his smart phone contacts. Also, as a general rule, allow your boss or the man who signs your paychecks to believe whatever he wants. Take comfort in knowing you're not the only one present who believes he's an ill-informed jackass. Let people enjoy their damn dinner.

People who claim to enjoy political debates are merely people trying to channel a highbrow outlet for battling. It's in a man's nature to compete, often just for the sport. Understand it as such and you will find it enrages you that much less. If you find yourself routinely engaged in political, or worse yet, religious, debates, it's probably time to reassess your social channels and use of your free time. A man greatly restricts the time he spends arguing over entirely subjective matters and even then the discussion ought to be about ranking the Bond films or SI swimsuit models.

A Man Knows How To Talk Sports

Sports are one of those topics that men perpetually either delve into far too deeply or far too lightly. Men have trouble finding that happy middle ground between the all-consuming sports fanaticism and "I don't really follow sports" mantras, neither of which are healthy or acceptable in the world of men.

MAN RULES

You need not be an expert on all sports; you must be conversant in the ones that matter. You can go ahead and forget about intricate rules of cricket or the subtleties of curling. But you should have a passing familiarity with the rules of baseball, football, basketball, hockey, and yes, even soccer. The world is getting smaller. Make general knowledge of major soccer events such as the World Cup part of your lexicon. Nobody said being a man was going to be easy.

It's important for a man to be able to easily communicate with other men in any given situation. Men are most comfortable talking about sports. Where Esperanto failed miserably as the universal tongue, discussions about the Super Bowl and World Series and NBA Finals blossomed into universal spoken language among men. Sports chatter in the West is akin to the open palms up sign to the ancient Masai of Africa, a gesture that you come in peace. We are friends. Let us now break chicken wings and discuss the outcome of sporting events we were never athletically inclined enough to participate in ourselves. Not all rules of men are entirely masculine.

Apprise yourself of the basics. You don't need to win trivia contests by naming Yogi Berra as the catcher for the '56 Yankees, but you should know roughly who the better teams are in baseball this year. When you walk into that big job interview and you notice that the guy has a signed Jeter baseball you should have something instantly to talk about. Sexism in hiring isn't so much a conspiracy as it is the fact that most women couldn't give a rat's ass that Derek Jeter ended his career top six in all-time hits. Tom Brady plays for the Patriots. LeBron James brought a championship to Cleveland finally. You took three semesters of political science that you will never ever find a practical application for in your post-collegial life. Memorizing fifty basic facts from the sporting world may provide you with enormous benefit by comparison.

Included in this general winners and losers knowledge must be the general rules and lingo of the sport. Know the difference between a touchdown, a homerun, and a game-tying three-pointer. The free throw line is in basketball, the red zone infers proximity to the goal in in football, and PEDs only sounds like a horrible crime, when in fact it just means the latest version of steroids ball players are consuming to gain an edge. Like most red-blooded Americans you might think soccer is stupid. Granted, but you should at least know that the only player who can use his hands is the goalie and the difference between a red card and a yellow card and how they apply to midfielders faking physiological trauma while writhing on the ground from feigned contact.

This isn't that much to learn. If you grew up in a household of guys, you probably inherently speak this language. If you didn't, or you rejected this heritage as foolish or oppressive, a quick half hour watching SportsCenter should provide you with enough to pass. When in doubt or caught up short, simply shrug and say "at least they left it all on the field" or "they just wanted it more" and make for the guacamole.

Men Do Not Chat on the Phone

Alexander Graham Bell invented the telephone almost one hundred and fifty years ago. The first phone call between two men went like this:

MAN RULES

Bell: *Does it work?*

Bell's Assistant: *Yeah it works.*

Bell: *Goodbye.*

The telephone was invented so information could be communicated quickly between two remote parties without having to tap out messages at the local public telegraph office. Imagine trying to hook up with your late night booty call by asking the Western Union clerk to dot and dash the phrase 'I'm coming over to plow my tongue into your dump cake. Stop.'

The phone was invented to get down to business. It was not made for chitchat. When you're on the phone, say what you have to say and you hang up. Any business that takes longer than two minutes should be conducted face-to-face, or lawyer-to-lawyer. Women may use the phone or similar devices as a form of entertainment. If a man seems amused while talking into the phone, you should alert the authorities. Though it's probably nothing, nothing more than him sacrificing his manhood.

It's not particularly manly to talk on the phone because it's like having another man's mouth in your ear, and your mouth in his ear. I'm not sure what you call that, but where I'm from, we call it a 1980's George Michael video. You do not want to find yourself in a 1980's George Michael video, unless you like snow and sexually suggestive overtones between men in Christmas sweaters. Despite what the guy at the mall kiosk says, adding a Bluetooth to the equation only magnifies the problem. You want to walk through life on wireless talking to your friends? You might as well just invite your buddy to the back row of a matinee at that point for a make-out session.

Everything becomes less manly when it's said on the phone. Even Clint Eastwood sounds like a pussy over the phone. 'What's it gonna be punk?' suddenly sounds like a neighborhood girl asking if you've found her lost kitty cat. Do you want to be the dude who sounds like a little girl asking about a lost kitty? Do you feel lucky? Well, do you?

Outside of dirty talk with your significant other, if you can get away with that, limit the length of your phone calls to just the facts and move on. Keep in mind why Bell invented this thing in the first place. If you find yourself constantly engaging in long, laugh-out-loud or gasping phone conversations, you should go get yourself some yoga pants and cancel your NFL TV package, because it is time to start your new life. If you lack self-control, destroy your phone now as an addict flushes his narcotic down the toilet to save himself. Yes, Candy Crush goes with.

BASIC SKILLS

A Man Knows How To Camp, Then Rarely Does

Man spent thousands of generations evolving out of the wilderness and into entirely safe and comfortable indoor abodes with thermostats that counter the grand forces of nature outside. There are a few of the modern tribe who feel a longing for reconnecting with their primal roots. They'll periodically insist on sleeping on the ground, risking inclement weather and puma attack, and digging a hole to shit in. Camping.

Camping seemed truly thrilling as a child because your other option was staying home and trying to figure out your parents' lockout code on your TV remote. Camping connoted something wild, adventurous, and even dangerous. Later you learned it was mostly just hauling bags, bickering over who forgot what, and waiting for it to be over so you could return to civilization and regale the soft city people with a completely hyperbolized account of your weekend.

Regardless of the purely symbolic nature, a man must make an outdoor pilgrimage once a year in order to truly appreciate the far more brilliant majesty of his flat screen. Think of it as your annual physical. You're not sick, but once a year you visit your doctor anyhow and pay him to confirm you're in the 50-percent bracket across the board.

If you're heading out for a guy trip for the holiday weekend, the process of getting on the highway is simple. You'll need a cooler with beer and meat, lighter fluid, bug spray, dope, and some camping chairs and tents. Keep in mind there's going to be a Wal-Mart within twenty minutes of your destination should someone forget their spare wood mulcher or black jack table. This is amateur camping. You want amateur camping. If you're a hardcore outdoorsman or survivalists, odds are you don't need this book in the first place.

Upon arriving at your campground, set up your tent, as this is at minimum a two-hour job akin to building a hot air balloon out of pick-up-sticks. If this vital chore is put off, you'll soon be drunkenly stabbing your tent to death as the shot clock expires on the sun. This will inevitably happen anyway so just call dibs on the car. It's airtight, relatively free of ants or spiders, and contains a trusty heater. If you kill the car battery, that's your fault but everybody's problem.

Once you return to home base from any hiking, fishing, or sneaking off to some bar filled with the grown up Children of the Corn, you'll need to set up the fire. Build it just large enough to frighten the wife, but not so big as to start a massive forest fire. If it can be seen from space you've gone too far. Try to remember you're wearing a North Face jacket. Cro-Magnon needed the fire. You just like the way the smell reminds you of your grandmother's at Christmas. The next morning your campsite will be littered with steak bones and scorched raccoons. A man cleans up after himself out of respect and also a deep fear of nature's wrath. If you get your head cracked open by a coconut in Maui next year, you'll know you missed a few cans of Pabst.

Having a woman in tow presents a different set of circumstances, as she'll be shoving over-the-counter medications and color-coordinated sun hats into the last cranny of your car. She'll insist you leave at three a.m. and by the time she finishes unpacking it will be dark the next day. She'll wake up cranky and mutter something about a decent hairdryer. This isn't a subtle message. She'd rather be staying in a hotel. If you have the means, this is where you drive to one immediately and spend the next day or two satisfying your organically invigorated libidos in the comfort of a pillow top bed.

There are many pleasures to be had enjoying nature, provided you plan and equip reasonably. You want to strike a balance between fugitive on the run and portable wine cellar. One or two nights and you'll feel like a new man. If for no other reason than you just consumed five weeks' worth of protein in one weekend.

Drink Like A Man. What's the Alternative?

Men don't drink because they delight in hints of oak or grapefruit. They drink because the basement flooded again. A man keeps his drinking simple. The more lemon peel the bartender has to grate into your specialty cocktail, the longer you're forced to converse with that longshoreman about his sore ankle. Hell, that bartender might actually be a mixologist, and your drink might be an aperitif. By the time you've looked that term up you've already taken to wearing gowns and calling yourself The Other Nancy.

A man's regular drink is beer. Not light beer. If you're counting calories, stop drinking beer. Also, stop counting calories. It's the only segment of mathematics dominated by women. Light beer has slightly fewer calories and slightly less alcohol, meaning more trips to the bathroom and a sign you lack control in the general reproductive region. Girls on Tinder are never seeking men with weak bladders.

A man may enjoy many styles of beer, most notably your more sturdy IPA's that taste like those pennies you find at the bottom of the washing machine. If you find yourself grimacing on first sip, you've found yourself a beer fit for a man. If you find yourself refreshed by notes of wolfberry, you're not consuming a beer; you're saying *auf Wiedersehen* to your manhood.

Drinking wine is acceptable in the appropriate setting. Perhaps when you're trying to impress your boss for a promotion or somebody is threatening to kill your family if you don't. There is no appropriate time for savoring. Savoring is something done by people who aren't obsessively thinking about all the trees in the world yet to be chopped down. Also, wine is fruit. You can't have fruit in your beer and you can't feel manly drinking a glass of juice. A man is inherently wary of things with stems on them. That includes the grapes and the wine glasses. Why not just pick a sunflower if you love stems so much? Do you see how slippery this slope is?

When choosing a hard drink, a man should drink whiskey. Men grit their teeth and howl at the moon. Whiskey neat helps in this regard. If you're Russian or making alcohol out of potato peels in prison, then vodka is acceptable. If you're considering a fruit mixer then you've not been reading closely and your odds of leading a band of renegades like Patrick Swayze in Red Dawn is minimal to none. Gin and rum are both fine if you want to shake hands with the devil or if you are having hot flashes.

A man never gets drunk to the point he can't maintain an erection or use that erection to beat other men. Nor does he remain sober to the point that he's annoyed that his friends are being drunk. He doesn't show up to the bar when it opens with his morning paper. He has two but not more than four drinks in a social setting intermixed with conversation and darts, remains under the legal blood alcohol driving limit, or gets home in a cab to think about what woman he can call that would be willing to watch Braveheart on his sofa for the fourth time.

Native Americans call alcohol firewater because it's as important as two of the four major earthly elements in terms of survival. Treat alcohol with respect and in turn, alcohol will treat you like a man.

A Man Forms His Own Opinions

Men have an understanding of the world around them and current events shaping that world. The notion of the uninvolved slacker with no time for thoughtful or informed discussion is anything but manly. That doesn't mean an intense immersion in news and information followed by social media rants filled with self-righteous certainty. It implies educating yourself to the point of being able to have opinions with some reasonable basis in fact. You are not a politician or a college professor or a magazine editorialist, but you are a man, and men have educated points of view. You can apply 20 to 30 minutes a day to making this so.

Having a grip on local, national, and world events will come in handy in the bar, on the golf course, or in a room with no windows should you happen to be detained by the Feds. Having a working command of current affairs is how men communicate and close deals. It's not about the specifics; it's more a litmus test of intellectual curiosity. When you meet a young lady's grizzled peg-legged father he may ask your opinion of an overseas conflict. Have an opinion. If you wish to receive his blessing for intercourse with his daughter, espouse an opinion likely to be in line with his own.

A man never bases his opinion on a conversation with a buddy. Guys are completely full of crap and will claim to be an expert in foreign policy after watching a segment of CNN in their dentist's waiting room. If you go around repeating stuff you've heard and passing it off as your own opinion someone will eventually embarrass you in a conversation circle. You deserve it for being lazy.

Often times other men will give you bum information to see if you'll actually believe their nonsense. Columbus defeated the Nazis? Let's see if he repeats that at the cocktail mixer.

When browsing current events, the cardinal rule is to do some reading. People who get their information solely from TV news are the same people who order a frying pan with a flashlight on it after watching an infomercial. The same holds for Facebook or YouTube. The great thing about social media platforms is anyone can upload a video. The bad thing about them is anyone can upload a video. There are almost zero respectable scholars who educated themselves on shared posts while eating Rice Krispy Treats.

There are very few even-keeled, objective journalistic outlets any longer. There never were many, now there are next to none. Everything you read is going to be slanted by corporate or personal opinion. You'll need more than a single reference to inform a well-rounded perspective. Eliminate the obvious BS from each source and proceed from there. Try to read articles that offer a point and counterpart within the same story. There are always two sides to every issue. It's naïve to believe they are always equal, but idiotic to be certain the other side does not exist or is not worthy of consideration.

Don't be the guy who nods along to conventional wisdom with the rubes at the bar. Think of unique takes on the news based upon your own study. Don't be swayed by the popularity of opinion. If that popularity extends to the very attractive woman you're currently courting, you can be swayed for one night. Business is business. But be sure to reveal your views to her on sub-Saharan strip mining before you get married.

Because you've familiarized yourself with a certain topic does not mean you should walk around town soliciting debates with the clerk at the liquor store. Everybody hates a blowhard. Keep the information in your back pocket for the appropriate setting. Showing up some blathering schmuck is always an appropriate setting. Unless you have personal experience with the subject, remain diplomatic. Anecdotal experience is vastly overrated as a means of argument, but it is almost universally accepted as superior. You're trying to blend in, not get your ass kicked by the dad with the peg leg.

A Real Man Earns The Remote

Things that plug into the wall are the purview of the man of the house. With ultimate power comes ultimately responsibility. You might pull the remote as

Arthur did the sword from the stone, but you are by no means king until you've shown the ability to rule over your dominion of household appliances and consumer electronics.

You can't just demand the remote because you are the one with the penis. You must understand how the remote works and how all the equipment is hooked up. Don't have the guy from the big-box store set up your home entertainment center unless you want your woman looking at him the way dog looks at a steak. He has brought fire whereas you are unable to even create a spark. We didn't get to the moon by allowing the less ambitious among us to be fruitful and multiply.

An audio-visual set up is one of the simplest forms of household construction. You're creating one single circuit. Inputs go into outputs from one device to the other. Most modern televisions or similar display devices also serve as the central receiver. A higher resolution picture like a Blu Ray should definitely go HDMI but a video game device can probably go component. This is the sum total of your decision-making on assembly and it's laid out in the instructions that you can read after everybody else is asleep and pretend you assembled it from instinct.

You should be the one in your house to master the universal remote. It should look like some kind of magic when you seamlessly switch from the Xbox to the Apple TV. Hermione is drawn to the powerful wand. Make yourself Harry Potter and feel the burn.

The same holds true for computers and mobile devices. A man should know how to deftly remove viruses, install software, or set up a modem and router. Taking a number at the Genius Bar signifies you are not the genius. Look around at all that failure. Take your computer to the shop when there is a hardware issue that requires replacement or micro soldering outside of your expertise, real or pretend. When in doubt, try turning it off and on again. If that doesn't work, take it outside and shoot it and go buy another one.

Never call a kid who weighs a buck twenty to come tame your equipment for you. A call to the Geek Squad indicates they've added you as a junior member. That's abject surrender. A man chooses death over such indignity, or declares he's living off the grid to avoid the humiliation ever again. The war between man and machine began long ago. The big change in the future will be when we start losing the war. Until the day the remote controls you, reign beneficently over the electronics in your home.

Men Are Their Own Exterminator

Unless termites are eating the entire house, you do not call the exterminator. That is your job. Back in ancient times men protected their women and kids from saber-toothed tigers or Assyrian shock troops. Today, we mostly have rats and roaches to deal with. A man laughs in the face of death. He can't rightfully be squeamish in the face of a miniscule creature that isn't packing.

When bugs rear their ugly heads, you must destroy them. Don't capture them in a cup and set them free. If you have a friend or co-worker who insists this is the humane thing to do, set bugs free in their home and measure their level of commitment. Vermin cannot be rehabilitated or reasoned with. Bugs are the enemy and they deserve no mercy. Your home is your castle. They were not invited into the castle. They are marauders, whether consciously or not. If you had 15,000 panda bear cubs living beneath your bathroom sink, you'd take action. Spilling blood, even adorable blood, is sometimes necessary to preserve civilization. If you allow bugs or rats to mate, you will soon have colonies of them feasting on the kindness you never offered.

Killing any living creature should not be fun for a man. Though the ability to take a life righteously is one measure of his manhood. Stare that bastard roach in its beady black soulless devil eyes and firmly stare, "You go no further. I send you back to hell!" and then crush its thorax under a rolled up copy of Guns & Ammo or your girlfriend's Elle magazine. Though do not confess to the latter.

If the kill fits inside a shoebox, it is your duty to dispose of them. Animal control may be called when you've killed, say, a wildebeest that got into your bougainvillea, but otherwise you're on the hook for the cleanup. Use whatever method is cleanest and quickest, but don't leave death lying around your home. There are a variety of modern traps, poisons, sprays, and other instruments of pest death. Extermination is gross. It's supposed to be gross. Dealing with gross stuff with a blank stare is what separates you from the gender allowed to wear leggings in public. You're not a delicate flower. You are the unbreakable root. Rack up some kills and you'll find your nightly slumber remarkably sedate.

5 Fix-It Skills Every Man Should Know

There are certain tasks that men might want to call a specialist in to do, such as installing a septic tank or defusing a bomb. A man should be able to perform more simple, routine fix-it and repair jobs himself. The number of grown men who don't even own a toolbox is shocking and a statistic you have to hope never gets into the hands of our enemies. Certainly there are more services than ever before to perform tasks on your behalf. Almost all of them are just a digital click away. But every time you dial up someone to engage one of these five inherently male tasks, your girlfriend subconsciously finds you less than masculine and your grandfather cries on the inside.

Change a tire. When you get a new or new used car, examine the manual and figure out where the tools and the spare are. When you get a flat you are invariably in an inconvenient spot like a freeway or an abandoned road filled with monsters. Simply loosen the nuts, jack up the car, take off the old tire, put on the spare, un-jack the car, tighten the nuts, and put the old tire where the spare was (if it can be repaired. If not, light it on fire and hightail it). Step by step, it's immensely simple. It requires very little physical strain. Not nearly as painful as feeling your testicles shrink when the AAA guy says "no problem" but he has that look like he's your older brother and you just told him you think girls are gross.

Drill a hole. Step one; possess a drill. Cordless drills are nice but unless you're going out on the road with your drill, choose one with a cord so you need not deal with battery issues. You should obtain a decent set of good screw heads and drill bits. If you can't drill a simple hole in your wall to hang a fixture, you need to ask yourself what better man will be drilling your girl by this time next week.

Fix a leak. A normal man should not be expected to tear out a wall and repair a major pipe break. But he should be able to get under the sink where water is dripping onto his Rogaine and his girl's tampons. Do not call a plumber. Realize where leaks come from. Get yourself a wrench and tighten the pipe and put some thread seal tape around the joint. If you can't Macgyver a simple leaky pipe, why, you're not Macgyver at all.

Sew a button. Back in the day men managed their own basic repairs on clothes like fixing a button or patching a small hole. What happens when you lose a button five minutes before the big meeting? You don't have time to call your mom or rush to the guy from Uzbekistan you count on to mend your fineries. Men are above all else self-sufficient. Keep a travel sewing kit in your desk or car.

Assemble furniture. Many men suffer from a lack of male confidence and can't even put together a Spørgen or a Glüfenschas from IKEA. You need not be able to build a table from a tree you felled yourself (though that would be awesome). But you must have the wherewithal to follow simple instructions to assemble pre-fab furniture that stays together until the next break up or until the kid grows out of it.

Men Are Either Always Ready or Moments Away

Readiness is close to manliness. A man never needs to check his watch to answer how long he needs to get ready. He was born ready. Asleep on the couch in his underwear beneath a newspaper and a wet dog means he's almost ready. The answer to the readiness question is one of two possibilities for a man: "let's do this" or, in dire circumstances, "give me just a minute". As to the latter, he does mean sixty seconds.

Women primp before ever leaving the abode, even to get the grocery store inserts from the mailbox. Primping has no specific time limit but the word connotes far more than sixty seconds. A full primping session includes but is not limited to: showering; shaving legs and armpits; drying their hair; putting on makeup; trying on multiple outfits that may or may not fit or look good, based upon prevailing winds and barometric pressure; and selecting accessories. Getting ready is not a destination for women; it's all about the journey. If you find a woman that is in the car within 45 minutes after the time she declares she needs to get ready, move in together. If she does it in 30 or less, put a baby in her and make it for forever.

Men have significantly less of a role in fine-tuning their superficial appearance. With less of a role comes less responsibility. However, a man must always make time to execute the holy trinity: shave, shower, and shit. Men have performed these three tasks expediently and managed to look good for generations. The holy trinity is fifteen minutes, never to be interrupted by checking scores on the phone or tugging one out just in case. Just in case of what has never been answered, but presumably this dates back to the height of the Cold War when the bomb might drop at any moment.

Men don't use "product". They shouldn't even use the word "product" unless they earn a paycheck as a hair care products distributor or they transship opium through the Khyber Pass. Men use shaving cream, shampoo (no conditioner), soap (not body scrub), aftershave or cologne (never both), and deodorant. That is it. No moisturizer, no tinted sunscreen, no eye cream, no body splash, no Axe body spray, and never eye makeup unless you are starring in a silent movie. It's always important to ask yourself the question, "Do I look beautiful?" Then slap yourself with some gusto and remind yourself that you're a man and this time ask, "Do I look not horrible?" You're good to go.

It's easy for a man to fall into the trap that the bathroom is his Fortress of Solitude. It's not. It's a toilet and a sink and a shower. You've already got a Man Cave, this is your Can Cave. A bathroom for men is simply another toolbox. Get what you need and get out. There's a woman with a mild-to-serious addiction to toiletries waiting to enter, and she's in withdrawal.

After the can, another five minutes is all you require to dress yourself, seven if you are wearing a suit. Unless you've been invited to the vacant church basement for a secret ancient trade association meeting, you do not need time to figure out what to wear. The very reason fancy events instruct you how to dress is to save the men any thinking. Women already know. A man puts on what is appropriate and feels good. Business meeting? Suit. Job as a blogger or graphic designer? Jeans and a clean shirt. A date? Maybe some khakis or your non-ripped jeans and a button down shirt. Take the time in the shower or while dropping a deuce to figure it out then execute like you're on the police response-clock during a bank heist.

From the moment you enter the bathroom until the time you leave the house should take no longer than 25 minutes, 30 if it's morning and you're taking the dog out to whizz and having breakfast. You have important stuff to do. Even if you don't, or you can't think of anything, repeat that phrase in your head while getting ready. It will prevent you from reading through the entire Tom Clancy library whilst on the shitter.

Every Man Should Know How To Play a Little Guitar

You don't need to play like Stevie Ray Vaughn reincarnated in your living room, simply know how to strum a song or two, just a song or two. It is a scientifically supported fact that women sleep with guitarists at a rate ten times that of non-guitarists. Can you fathom how many attractive ladies Keith Richards has explored in his 800 years on Earth? Master a couple of songs to keep in your repertoire. Should you find yourself in the proximity of a girl and a guitar you'll be ready. Say you bring a girl over to your place to show her your new book on 19th Century romantic oil paintings. She notices the guitar you have leaning awesomely against a wall.

Girl: Oh, you play guitar?
You: Oh, yeah. I play a little. Nothing great.
Girl: Play me something…

Hem and haw twice more then smile and break out Chris Isaac's "Wicked Games". You won't get through the song with your pants on. Pick something a girl might actually like to hear. Stay away from anything by GWAR or The Insane Clown Posse. This isn't cheating. You took the time to learn. She took the time to undress. There's something about guitar like no other handcrafted tool a man can ever hold.

It's easy to learn a simple, first-position chord, and many popular numbers only contain three. "Battleship Chains" contains two. Three of the easiest chords to master are G, D, C - the unholy blues trinity. With these three chords you can play hundreds of songs from Johnny Cash's "Ring of Fire" to Lynyrd Skynyrd's "Sweet Home Alabama" to AC/DC's "You Shook Me All Night Long".

Drums are also an acceptable instrument to play, as drummers have toned arm muscles, are hardcore and die prematurely, which women find attractive in a man, especially with a jumbo life insurance policy. If you play piano, you had better be able to set it on fire and smash it like Jerry Lee Lewis. Everything else is just your first grade teacher playing BINGO on the upright. Harmonica is easy, cheap, and transportable, and also fits nicely into the pervasive belief among women that harmonica players provide excellent oral copulation. The science is still out.

Singing is not playing an instrument, it's talking pretty. Just because you think you can sing after a half dozen Jaegers on karaoke night doesn't mean you can. Chances are you can't. Never sing for a woman until a record industry executive has invested money in your voice. That'll be the sign it's okay to proceed.

A Man Knows How to Order A Beer

You can't trust a man who doesn't like beer. The same broad-brush judgment holds true for men who don't have a favorite sports team. You don't have to be pre-occupied with beer or consume it daily to affirm your affinity, but any man who doesn't enjoy the occasional cold one is a man without a solid center. These are men who talk about staying "present", and discuss "sitting" with their "feelings". Don't ever put them in the care of your dog. They will surprise you upon your return by insisting your dog has chosen a vegan lifestyle.

Even if you're largely indifferent to beer you should develop a basic understanding of the universally popular beverage. Nobody will fault you for appreciating wine with a good meal. But you cannot order a Sauvignon Blanc at the local dive and expect to keep cave privileges.

For better or worse, the days of ordering a Budweiser in the local pub are basically over. Even your crappier watering holes with a pickled egg jar and a bartender who once killed a man carry twenty brews from coastal Oregon with contrived brand names. Rest assured half of them taste like a dirty sweat sock stuffed with coins.

Your nineteen-year-old server isn't interested in providing you a scientific lecture on IBUs. You need to learn the basics. Lagers and pilsners are going

THE BEGINNER'S GUIDE TO MANHOOD

to taste like a normal beer. An IPA is going to taste like a strong beer, a Hefewiezen like a rotten beer, stouts and porters like a bowl of cereal. Look at the alcohol content and bitterness ratings on the menu and gauge how adventurous you're feeling. American beer used to be largely lower in liquor proof than beer from foreign nations where they sip, rather than chug through funnels. That is no longer always the case. Don't assume you need to shotgun six beers to get buzzed. Read the labels if you don't want to be up on a chair shrieking for more Ozzy an hour into your evening.

Half the men in your modern pubs are beer nerds toting their own forensic kits to test for various impurities in the cherry wood. Their love of beer is matched only by their love of talking about their love of beer. Even if you've never met before, they will give you a stellar recommendation after a 15-minute debriefing on aspects of your life even a professional shrink couldn't get out of you in two years of sessions. Proceed with caution. You get the wrong beer and he's inviting you back to his shack in the woods to look at his yeast starter. There's no shame in asking the bartender, 'What do you like?' or 'What is popular?' Men shouldn't feel threatened by people who know more about a given subject than they do, except for cars and martial arts. Definitely not pale ale.

Beer is a rare area of study where knowing just the basics is preferable to having a doctorate. Beer was invented for sitting around and talking about women and sports, not discussing hops and malts. Beer snobs are boring. Many a curious hobbyist has turned that corner, and when it happens it's ugly. Before you know it you're ordering off menu or bringing your own special cup with you or correcting the bartender's terminology. It's better to be ignorant than universally disliked. Find a beer you like and stick with it. That's how a man turns a pure whim into his usual. Get this simple thing right.

A Man Knows a Few Parlor Tricks

There are certain skills and areas of knowledge that separate a man from somebody grasping for the same status. Feeling outclassed in a social setting can lead to unexplained fits of road-rage the following day. These small investments of your time will pay vast dividends and help insure your virility and mental health.

Be passable at billiards and/or darts. There is something undeniably cool about sinking an 8-ball or hitting a bull's-eye. Don't be the guy holding the cue like a fish stick. There's no shame in losing to a shark, but there is in looking like you've been in prep school since birth. You want to suspend disbelief to the point of saying, "Well played. You got me this time," with a straight face.

Take some time to learn about wine. A few hours of knowledge that rarely needs updating. This one is good with fish, this one with steak. Hints of oak, spice, or fruit. It's not rocket science. When a lady comes back to your house she might not bite on Long Island iced tea and Tostitos. Uncorking a bottle of wine signifies class. Think of it as less clumsy foreplay. Don't cheap out on the price. A reasonably cost-benefit analysis will show you why it's a better investment than the sneakers you bought promising yourself you'd start jogging again.

<u>Get a Zippo</u>. Even if you don't smoke, leave the house with a metal lighter in your pocket. Women often smoke as an excuse to talk to strangers. Asking for a light initiates conversation. You may not want to marry a smoker, but this isn't marriage, this is your buddy's apartment-house luau. Flipping open a lighter with the flick of a wrist provides you with Bogart-level allure and Vietnam-vet toughness. Besides, someone has to light the tiki torches.

<u>Learn one bar trick.</u> Guys who turn any public space into an amateur magic show are insufferable and go to their grave never having known the scent of a woman. Their level of mastery reveals the amount of free time they have in their lives. Holding one skill in your back pocket easily displayed from a bar stool can be an instant icebreaker. It can be as simple as folding a dollar bill into the shape of a grouse. She's not looking for perfection, just a sign of Renaissance.

<u>Learn how to open bottles with the most meager of tools.</u> Prying open a beer bottle with a lighter is compulsory and should be taught in grade school. Another reason to carry a Zippo. There's nothing worse than not having a corkscrew and running around in increasingly tighter concentric circles waiting for Jesus to lower one from the sky to save the evening. If your solution involves a machete, you've made her pregnant just through desire.

<u>Learn how to cook a few dishes from scratch.</u> There are more male chefs in this world than female. Men are by nature drawn to cooking. Slaughtered boars didn't roast themselves. Take the time to learn how to prepare a few unexpected meals. You will impress everybody in your life. You also won't

need a frequent diner card to eleven take-out joints. It's healthier, less expensive, and you will have more sex. This shouldn't need convincing.

Understand the basics of pugilism. Fighting is for drunken sailors and the sexually frustrated. But there are four billion men on this planet and the odds still remain decent one of them will engage you in a physical altercation at some time. You don't need to wreck him while laying verbal waste to his ancestors, you merely need to defend yourself and get few shots in long enough for mall security to come break it up. Find a guy at the gym who's in his 50's with a great deal of scarring on his face who's hitting the heavy bag. Explain that your father was absent in your life growing up and could he possibly show you a few pointers. He will spend the next six years turning you into Rocky.

Understand games of chance. Betting is a manly art, not a whimsical guessing game. Consider the elements of your wager. At some point in your life you'll find yourself in front of a blackjack table. Asking the dealer the rules of the game is an utter embarrassment, which is why casino hotels have entire TV channels explaining them. Like masturbation, rudimentary learning is embarrassing and should be done alone in your room. Understand the basic of table gaming, sports book making, and horse racing. You don't have to be a master, or even bet, just be able to explain it knowledgably to your girlfriend.

Know how to handle a weapon. There are a large number of guns in this country. Even if you have no desire to be near a gun, one will ultimately be near you. This may be a lawful firearm moment or one that results from a panicked lawless moment. In either event, it's best to be generally acquainted with guns, their safety, their storage, and their use. Marksman training is for hunters. You would be fine knowing the basic operating mechanisms and learning how not to break your wrist or blow your face off should you need to discharge on at some time in your life.

Know the score of the big game. Sports fanaticism is a spectrum. You don't want to be on either end of the curve. You don't need to carefully follow spectator sports, but you should be able to hold a brief and intelligent conversation on the meaningful games throughout the year. The Super Bowl, the World Series, the NBA Finals. If more than forty million people are watching, there's a good chance it will come up at the office or backyard party. "What did you think of the game?" is the male equivalent of women asking one another, "How are you doing?" It's a launching point into a tête–à–tête. You can't claim ignorance. You've just killed the relationship.

A Man Does Not First Ask Somebody Else What They're Having When Ordering

It is not that a man doesn't care what everyone else at the table is ordering, it is that a man is confident enough in his own food order that he doesn't need to know what anyone else is ordering before placing his own.

A man who can't decide what to eat is a man no woman would want. If you can't independently decide so much as a meal choice, how will you decide where to build her and your offspring a two-story Tudor? Will she have to constantly encourage you to be bold and stand up for yourself when the guys at work are calling you some effeminate version of your real name? No woman wants to do that, and no woman should have to do that. Don't be indecisive. Indecisive men are weak men.

Ordering etiquette may not seem like a big deal, but it is an indicator of a bigger problem. A man who is afraid to make the first move at dinner is likely to be afraid to make the first move in the bedroom. Whether ordering a steak, or convincing your mate she'd look amazing underneath you, a man needs to be confident. You can't turn to the bed next to you and ask somebody else how they intend to bang their lady before you entertain your own, so you shouldn't ask someone else what they are having to eat before your order.

Ordering dinner is not something to fear. It's the simple decision of what you will have for your next meal. You're going to have more meals. If you're on Death Row, maybe this is your last meal, but you still don't get to ask everyone else about to be executed what they were thinking of having. You don't want to leave this life as a lesser man.

You could order the same thing as someone else to be safe. But ask yourself this. Did the Neanderthal hunter ask his fellow spearman what game he was going to hunt that day before he headed out into the bush himself? No, he was hungry so he bled out whatever living creature moved in his path. Think about your more manly ancestors the next time you're at Carrows wavering between the hot turkey plate and the grilled ham and cheese sandwich and asking 'Steve' what looks good to him. Because what looks good to Steve right now is your woman.

A Man Understands Basic Survival

When the Independence Day aliens arrive or the undead comeback to life, your lady is going to look to you for help. What are you going to say, "Hang on, honey, I'm searching WebMD to see how to treat that unholy severed limb." She's going to leave your ass for a man who can protect her. And she should. Feminism takes a holiday when there's a natural disaster or a spider to be squashed.

Like a boy scout, a grown man should be able to perform basic outdoor survival skills like start a fire or navigate using the sun. It's also crucial to know a few first aid techniques like tying a tourniquet and sucking the poison from a snakebite. It doesn't take an apocalyptic event to require you know how to survive. What if you run out of gas in a secluded area or your girlfriend steps on a nail on that deck you've been meaning to fix. A man is always prepared.

Are these rules cliché? Possibly. Will they save a real life? Also quite possibly.

A man always carries a knife. There was a time when no gentleman left home without a trusty knife. You don't need a Bowie knife on your hip in 21st-century city living, but get yourself a nice multi-tool or Swiss Army knife with a variety of components. Like Jack Bauer, you can do anything with this little hunk of plastic and metal. With even a smaller knife you can cut tinder, cleave bandages, even tie it to a stick and make a spear. Keep it on you all the times unless you going through an airport. Then you will be sodomized by another man's gloved hand. And you'll lose your knife. You don't need either of those.

A man knows how to start a fire. Fire can mean the difference between life and death. Not only does combustion provide warmth, it provides fuel for cooking food and boiling your water to avoid dysentery. Diarrhea kills far more people than wild boar attacks annually. It's not even close. If you have a broken bottle shard you can do the old magnifying glass thing with the sun and ignite some moss, twigs, or crumbled up paper. If no glass is available, you can start a fire by rubbing some steel wool on a battery or by using a thin stick to drill a hole in another stick and waiting for friction to shoot a spark. If all else fails, you can touch the ends of jumper cables together while they are attached to your car battery. If that fails, watch for the boars.

A man knows how to tie a tourniquet. If you, or someone you are with, cuts themselves deep enough to hit an artery, they can bleed out quickly. Blood loss, or the prevention thereof, is most often the difference between life and death of the wounded. Doctors can mend and sew body parts back together. They can't do anything for the patient who lost a ton of blood on the way to their hospital. A tourniquet that slows blood loss is essential. Tear off a piece of cloth or use a piece of rope or anything of substance that can bind. Wrap it around the limb two or three inches above the wound. Tie and cinch as tight as you can. You are trying to stem the blood flow heading from the heart to the laceration. Tying too tightly, or leaving a tourniquet on for a long period, can result in loss of the limb, so only do this if there is a real possibility of death from blood loss. If possible, clean the open wound with some alcohol, vinegar, or other disinfectant. Press another makeshift bandage to the wound itself and apply steady pressure. You just saved your friends life. Welcome to Mount Man.

A man can open canned goods without a can opener. If power goes off and refrigeration isn't available, canned food is your best bet. Food that is properly canned can sit almost indefinitely and has saved many a person's life in time of crisis. If no commercially constructed can opener is available, produce your trusty pocketknife and a stand-in hammer and use it to poke holes around the lid of the can around the edges. If you lost your knife killing a bear or something, a nail will also do the trick. Boil the nail first with that fire-starting trick you learned earlier. Tetanus is not something you want for dinner. Though tetanus infection won't show up for up to two weeks. If you haven't eaten during that time, you'll have bigger concerns. The lip of the can lid can also be worn down on rough stone or concrete. Rub the lid back and forth until you see moisture on the rock indicating the seal is thin and breaking. It takes a while and you'll probably burn more calories than you consume, but man up, the family's having pork and beans as the city burns in the backdrop.

A Man Owns Tools

No man is an island. But every man should be able to survive more than an hour stranded on an island. You need not be a trained survivalist or skilled craftsman, but a man ill-prepared for basic repair and maintenance of his own dwelling is no man at all. If you can't care for your own home, how can you care for a mate and offspring, let alone protecting your clan in time of Visigoth pillage?

Men should take no part in the collection of gadgets. In the time you spent rooting around the garage for that patented infomercial towel, you could have washed the windows of every house in the neighborhood with your spare pallet of worn out undershirts. A man is above all else, resourceful. Organization skills may be limited. They can't be non-existent. Keep a limited number of essentials in a closet or garage space and know how to use them. You will feel a masculine pride you've never felt before and finally understand that a man doesn't get sex, he earns it.

Basic tool set. This would include multiple sized wrenches, two screwdrivers, pliers, a ballpeen hammer, and tape measure. Home Depot packs this all into a pre-set kit so you need not ask a man in an apron to teach you how to be a man. The expense should be no more than a couple hundred dollars. But you need to spend a couple hundred dollars. You bought a $200 Ikea coffee table that came in a matchbox. Don't compound the issue by employing the Fisher Price tool set they include for assembly.

Medium-sized ladder. Animals live in shelters that barely contain their height and girth. Humans choose to dwell in structures notably larger than their minimum sleeping and breeding needs. You're not supposed to be able to reach your ceiling or climb easily onto your roof. Fixtures, tiles, and shingles are all beyond your reach. Stacking phonebooks under chairs is not an answer. Get a foldable ladder. It need not be fire rescue ready to the tenth floor. A six-foot stepladder will do for the vast majority of your elevating needs.

Toilet Plunger. A clogged toilet should not have to be announced at a party before asking everybody to please file out of your home in an orderly fashion. A man should be able to plunge a toilet and properly fix basic breakdowns in the tank. Knowing how to re-assemble the toilet ballcock makes you manlier, ironically. A simple drain snake is only a few bucks and will save you hundreds but probably above and beyond the normal course of duty. A man who snakes his own drains is welcome in Valhalla.

Basic painting supplies. You can't call yourself a man if you're calling upon another man to touch up scratches and chips around your living quarters. Would you call a stand-in to help your wife zip up her dress? Nobody expect you to do a full multi-coat exterior around your structure, but if you can't touch up cabinets and doors and paint over the Pokémon your nephew drew on the wall, then you're one step away from hiring college guys to come into your home to move the couches. God spent some decent time making you. Don't make him watch you search Yelp for somebody to wipe your bottom.

Power drill and nail gun or staple gun. Guys who rip phone books in half can break into tears trying to get a screw into a stud. You're a mid-career marketing manager. You don't need racks of power tools. But you must have a power drill. You will use it no more than three to four times a year but you will use it proudly. The same is true of a nail gun. If you're only in need of basic hanging and repair, a staple gun will hold up most everything until you move. Don't overlook the weaponry uses of a nail gun. Always best to put it into a locked cabinet that requires a Breathalyzer test to open.

MAN RULES

<u>Utility knife</u>. There was a day and age when a man was never without a knife on his hip. Unless you live beneath a thatched roof and the bears keep stealing your winter stores, you probably don't require a survival knife. A Swiss Army Knife or Leatherman Utility Knife remains forever useful. Not for mortal combat, but so you're not left prying and ripping things apart with your keys or fingers. A man doesn't reach for the scissors when his Amazon box arrives with the Godfather DVD collection. Deftly reach into your pocket and slice that box open. Now you deserve the favor of your Don.

<u>Lighter</u>. What you should or should not be able to accomplish as an adult male in the outdoors in regard to fire is one matter, endlessly searching for old bar matches in drawers is another. Fire is essential to man. You should never be more than ten seconds way from being able to successfully create combustion. If you don't smoke, you need not carry a lighter on your person, but you better have a decent Bic and a solid set of waterproof matches within easy reach. The tribe has a name for the man who allows the fire to die. Meat.

<u>WD-40</u>. Structures and fixtures are no different than people. They require lubrication. Whether for her pleasure or yours, a man always has an aerosolized can of mineral oil ready to unsqueak, unstick, and unrust every possible interaction of moving parts under his roof. WD-40 is the offline version of fixing your computer by turning it off and back on again. It's what you must try first before signing up for any costly repair.

<u>Crowbar</u>. Sometimes a man needs to rip and destroy things. Much less often than he'd let on, but when the situation arises you do not want to be left

looking for your souvenir baseball bat. Think of a crowbar as your modern day sword. Now stop thinking of that because you're merely using it to pry open a window you accidentally painted shut. Your buddy has the same issue and he's just destroyed a table fork. You may now sleep with his girlfriend. Strap the crowbar to your back and whoop.

Sawzall. Whether you're cutting an ambitious sandwich in half or taking down the Sequoia in the front yard, you're covered with a cordless reciprocating saw. Get the smallest one you can find. You don't have an ox named Babe. You're cutting a breathing hole in the doghouse you assembled incorrectly. A man is often defined by how long it takes to complete a ten second job. Aim for ten seconds.

The Beginner's Guide to Manhood

L E X   J U R G E N

Roehampton Road Press
LOS ANGELES

Made in the USA
Middletown, DE
14 October 2016